GARBAGE
AND
RECYCLING

Kathlyn Gay

—Issues in Focus—

ENSLOW PUBLISHERS, INC.

Bloy St. & Ramsey Ave.   P.O.Box 38
Box 777   Aldershot
Hillside, N.J. 07205   Hants GU12 6BP
U.S.A.   U.K.

Library of Congress Cataloging-in-Publication Data

Gay, Kathlyn.
 Garbage and recycling / Kathlyn Gay.
 p. cm. — (Issues in focus)
 Includes bibliographical references and index.
 Summary: Examines the problem of garbage accumulation in America
and different recycling solutions which may prevent the situation
from getting worse in the future.
 ISBN 0-89490-321-7
 1. Refuse and refuse disposal—United States—Juvenile literature.
2. Recycling (Waste, etc.)—United States—Juvenile literature.
[1. Refuse and refuse disposal . 2. Recycling (Waste)] I. Title
II. Series: Issues in focus (Hillside, N.J.)
TD788.G39 1991
363.72'8'0973—dc20   91-7130
                                                             CIP
                                                              AC
Printed in the United States of America

10 9 8 7 6 5 4 3 2 1

Photo Credits:
Aluminum Company of America, pp. 32, 33; American Paper Institute, p. 29;
American Petroleum Institute, p. 51; Douglas Gay, p. 28; Kathlyn Gay, pp. 8, 12,
19, 38, 53, 57, 72, 76; Institute of Scrap Recycling Industries, Inc., p. 41; The
Plastic Bottle Institute, p. 63; U.S. Geological Survey, p. 87.

Illustration Credit: Kathlyn Gay, pp. 15, 17.

Cover Photo:
Kathlyn Gay

Contents

1 Throwaway Societies 5
2 Recycling: The Closed Loop 14
3 Recycling Paper, Glass, and Cans 24
4 Scrap Isn't Junk 35
5 Putting Waste to Work 44
6 Problems With Plastics 55
7 Managing Hazardous Waste 64
8 Debates Over Nuclear Waste 78
9 The Environmental Decade 92
   Notes by Chapter 104
   Further Reading 108
   Groups to Contact 120
   Glossary 123
   Index 126

The garbage Americans throw away each year could cover 1,000 football fields, rising 30 stories high.

1
—
Throwaway Societies

Q. How many trees are used each week to produce the Sunday edition of U.S. newspapers that are not recycled?

A. About 500,000

Q. Each person in the United States throws away how many pounds (on average) of garbage and trash per day?

A. 3–4 pounds

Q. How much does it cost U.S. taxpayers to clean up litter from our national parks?

A. $15 million per year

Q. What do Rocky Flats, Colorado; Fernald, Ohio; and Oak Ridge, Tennessee, have in common?

A. They are all sites for nuclear weapons plants that produce highly radioactive waste.

These questions may look as though they came from a trivia game, but they reflect a serious problem in the United States and around the world: what to do with an ever-increasing amount of solid waste—trash and garbage. In addition, hazardous chemical wastes and nuclear wastes accumulate, posing health and environmental problems.

Few places are able to escape the problem of waste disposal. Garbage chokes waterways in many developing nations, and hikers and bikers trash mountainsides in such remote areas as the Alaskan wilderness and the Himalayas in India and Tibet.

Industries in both western countries and most eastern European countries generate tons of refuse every day, much of it hazardous chemicals, some of it nuclear waste. For example, "In an average year, British people discard more than 80 million tonnes (88 million short tons) of mixed household, commercial, and industrial wastes," according to a report in *New Scientist.*[1]

Each kind of waste requires a different method of disposal and treatment, some of which will be discussed in this book. But first, take a look at the kind of waste that everyone generates on a daily basis—garbage—or solid waste, as it is called.

The Garbage Crisis

People in the United States produce more waste than any other society in the world. In one year, for example, Americans throw out 1.6 billion disposable pens, 240 million tires, 2 billion disposable razors and blades, and about 18 billion disposable diapers. Enough aluminum is discarded each year to rebuild all of the commercial airplanes in the United States—every three months.

In just one metropolitan area, Los Angeles County, the garbage produced every nine to ten days would fill Dodger Stadium. The daily flow of solid waste from New York City is 27,000 tons. Each Chicagoan produces between five and six pounds of garbage daily. The refuse from other major cities and smaller communities brings the nation's total garbage heap from industrial, commercial, and residential sources to an estimated 250 million tons annually. Of that total, commercial and residential waste accounts for 160 million tons.

It would take a lineup of trucks reaching halfway to the moon to hold all the garbage generated each year by American consumers![2]

Where does all that stuff go? In the past, communities got rid of their garbage by tossing it into a river and letting the water carry the refuse downstream. As urban areas developed, people threw their garbage into an open dump at the edge of town. These dump sites attracted rats and other pests and eventually were outlawed. Today, municipal or private trash collectors haul garbage away and dispose of it in a landfill, areas that local governments have set aside for waste disposal and decomposition.

A landfill usually begins as an excavated area or pit. Garbage is dumped in the pit and covered over with a layer of soil. Bacteria in the soil can biodegrade, or break down, materials such as food scraps in a relatively short time. Decomposed materials then become part of the earth. But bacteria need oxygen and water to work efficiently. At most modern landfills, machines crush and tightly compact refuse, then pack down the dirt cover. Thus, the rate of decomposition slows down, and refuse may stay intact for many months or years. A milk carton can last five years; nylon cloth may be around for thirty to forty years; aluminum cans take from two hundred to five hundred years to decompose; and some glass and plastics may last millions of years.

Not only do these materials add to the heaps of waste that fill up disposal sites, but an increasing amount of trash contains toxic substances such as weed and pest killers, cleaning fluids, paint strippers, and used car oil. Some throwaways contain heavy metals like lead and mercury, proven health hazards. Lead may seep from corroding batteries, for example. Children exposed to low levels of lead can suffer brain damage, nervous system disorders, and other developmental problems.

Toxic compounds become part of the leachate, the liquid that percolates through or seeps from solid waste as it decomposes. If a landfill is not properly designed, leachate can run off into streams or seep through the soil into groundwater, the source of drinking water for at least half of the U.S. population. This is a particular problem in

7

areas where there are high levels of precipitation and soils are sandy and porous.

In 1976, the U.S. Congress passed the Resource Conservation Recovery Act that requires states to construct safer landfills. New ones must be underlined with thick layers of clay or vinyl materials or both, so that leachate will not percolate through the soil. In some areas, landfills can be constructed on clay beds that are a natural part of the land; in other areas, layers of clay soil must be laid down and compacted. However, only about 900 of the 6,000 landfills in the United States are lined.

In a well-designed landfill, layers of soil or synthetic materials cover the solid waste so rain and snow melts do not seep through. The

In most communities, garbage and trash collectors pick up the waste, haul it to a landfill, where the throwaways are covered over with dirt and compacted. Well-designed landfills have safeguards to prevent toxic materials from seeping into soils and waterways.

landfill also is built so that leachate can be trapped at the bottom and then drained off through pipes. Then waste water may be hauled away in tanker trucks to sewage treatment plants or stored on site for treatment to remove contaminants.

Gases that are generated when solid waste decomposes also must be controlled. One of those gases is methane, which is flammable. Methane can spread through the soil and seep into basements of nearby buildings, causing explosions. Several years ago, in Madison, Wisconsin, for example, methane seeped underground from a closed landfill into a nearby townhouse. The gas ignited, and the building exploded, injuring two tenants. After the accident, a system to control the gas was installed. A control system usually consists of vertical pipes sunk into the landfill to allow gases to escape. Sometimes the gas is collected and burned for energy.

Shipping Trash

Because of more strict standards for municipal landfills and the increasing amount of trash generated, many communities have had to close their waste disposal sites. Waste management experts predict that by the year 2000, only about one-third of the present landfills—perhaps 2,150—still will be open. New Jersey, for example, strictly regulates its landfills and closed more than 400 disposal sites during the 1980s.

Some New Jersey counties now are building huge incinerators to burn their solid waste. Until the burners are completed, state law requires trash haulers to take their cargo to a transfer station, where officials compact and measure the amount of garbage, which is then shipped by truck to sites in such states as Pennsylvania, Ohio, Kentucky, and Indiana. As a result, waste haulers must spend more to transport and dispose of garbage and trash. To avoid rising costs, some private haulers have dumped garbage "in parks, schoolyards, vacant lots, shopping center dumpsters and even bins belonging to the Salvation Army," according to a report in *The New York Times*.[3]

9

Rising costs affect trash haulers in most states, and one businessman, Lowell Harrelson, thought he had discovered an economical way to dispose of waste. In March 1987, he loaded 3,100 tons of garbage from Islip, New York, on a barge and planned to ship it to a site in North Carolina, where the garbage would be converted to methane gas. But Harrelson had not obtained approval from North Carolina. State officials suspected the garbage might contain hazardous materials and would not allow the New York barge to unload its cargo.

The barge traveled from port to port along U.S. coasts and even to Mexico and the Bahamas. Nobody would allow the garbage to be unloaded. After twenty-three weeks the barge returned to New York harbor, where the stuff, now reeking and covered with flies, was finally burned in a Brooklyn incinerator. The ash was buried in an Islip landfill, but not before the material was inspected and found free of hazardous materials.

"NIMBY" They Say

It is not difficult to see why the New York garbage barge became a dramatic symbol for the problems facing waste management specialists in western nations. A picture of the loaded barge at sea appeared with numerous magazine and newspaper articles about waste disposal problems. People want something done about the solid waste they generate, but "not in my backyard," as they say, a situation that has become known as the NIMBY syndrome.

NIMBY has been the rallying cry in the nation's midsection as solid waste from heavily populated eastern states is trucked into private Midwestern landfills. The state of Ohio, for one, would like more federal controls on garbage hauled across state lines. As one official pointed out, Ohio landfills are rapidly filling up, and trash from other states has doubled the volume of Ohio's solid waste materials. Ohio wants to limit interstate trash shipments by imposing high taxes on each ton imported. But states cannot tax or ban garbage since it is considered a commodity, like computers and other manufactured goods, and can be transported freely across state lines.

Imports of out-of-state trash have outraged people in a small community in central Indiana. It all began with Terri Moore, who lives with her family on acreage bordering a new Center Point Landfill in Clay County. Moore became concerned when the landfill opened in 1988 about one-half mile from a lake on her family's land. Her worries increased when she noticed that out-of-state trucks were rumbling past her home on the way to the landfill. A little investigating turned up the fact that the landfill, once locally owned, had been sold to a New Jersey waste disposal firm. The firm also had opened two other landfill sites in central Indiana.

Worry turned to indignation and anger when Terri Moore learned that the state of Indiana had issued a permit allowing the Center Point Landfill to accept hazardous materials. According to a report in the *Indianapolis Star*, the landfill logged in over seven cubic yards of hazardous asbestos in one month—most of it from New Jersey and Pennsylvania.

Armed with information about the content of the out-of-state waste, Moore talked to neighbors and friends who agreed to form HOPE (Hoosiers Opposing Pollution of the Environment). The group set up a daily "dump patrol" to monitor the trucks coming in and record license plates and names of at least 140 different hauling companies. Moore told reporters that the information is a protective measure—HOPE will know who is liable if anyone suffers health problems in the future due to toxic materials leaking from the landfill.

Former and present owners of the Center Point Landfill say that the geology—a natural clay underliner that prevents seepage—makes the area safe for disposal of wastes, including asbestos. The owners claim that asbestos is not mobile in soil so will not contaminate groundwater.

Apparently, the Indiana landfill meets state and federal regulations for waste disposal sites. However, Governor Evan Bayh and many Indiana legislators are working on ways to limit the amount of trash that will be accepted from out of the state. One possible solution would be to charge out-of-state haulers higher fees to dump garbage in Indiana landfills.

Along with health hazards posed by landfills, people also oppose land disposal of waste (no matter how safe the site might be) because of the social stigma. Living near a municipal landfill is equivalent, many believe, to living next door to a slum. The town dump has long been associated with those who have had to scavenge to survive. Most people consider garbage or trash collection an undesirable job, and

A trash collector at work.

even though municipal waste collectors may earn better-than-average incomes, their work relegates them to low status in the community.

Nevertheless, some landfills will always be needed, say waste management specialists, since the amount of trash continues to grow along with increases in population. Waste also illustrates a related problem. Nonrenewable natural resources are being used up at an alarming rate to produce countless consumer goods. In their book *Blueprint for a Green Planet*, authors John Seymour and Herbert Girardet put it this way:

> We are living on nature's capital instead of its income. In nature, production exactly matches consumption. Everything that grows eventually decomposes; the death and decay of one being becomes the precondition for the life of another. But our industrially based lifestyle, on the other hand, consists of loose ends. Raw materials are converted into consumer products, and these are not recycled. Instead they end up as sources of pollution.[4]

To protect and renew the earth, Seymour and Girardet, along with many others concerned about our throwaway societies, believe that conservation must be practiced worldwide. In industrialized nations, we need to observe the three Rs: recycling, reusing, and reducing waste at its source.

Every hour, Americans toss out 2.5 million plastic bottles;
only a small percentage are recycled.

2

Recycling: The Closed Loop

"If we could recycle just ten or eleven percent of what comes in here, we could extend the life of our landfill by six or seven years," said Tom Wilson, manager of a Midwest landfill. The percentage that Wilson cited represents the portion of total trash the United States recycles each year. But the U.S. Environmental Protection Agency (EPA) has set a higher goal. At least 25 percent of the nation's solid waste should be recycled by the mid-1990s, the federal agency says. However, the U.S. goal does not compare favorably with the recycling efforts already going on in Japan, where between 50 and 60 percent of the nation's waste is recycled. Nations in Western Europe recycle about 30 percent of their trash.

Separating materials is one of the first steps in the recycling process. In the United States, paper and paperboard, including packaging materials, account for an estimated 36 percent of all waste. Another 20 percent is yard waste—grass clippings, leaves, twigs, and similar materials. Metals and glass make up about 9 percent each of U.S. refuse. Another 9 percent of the garbage is food, and a little more than 7 percent is plastics. Other refuse includes wood products, leather, rubber, and fabrics.[1]

In a true recycling program, collected materials have to be processed—cut up, shredded, or prepared in some way for shipment, then fabricated or reused in another manufacturing process to make finished goods. Thus, if a new product such as a bicycle contains materials that have been reused, only then has recycling in its true sense been accomplished.

Demand for Recyclables

To recycle such materials as paper, glass, metals, and fabrics,

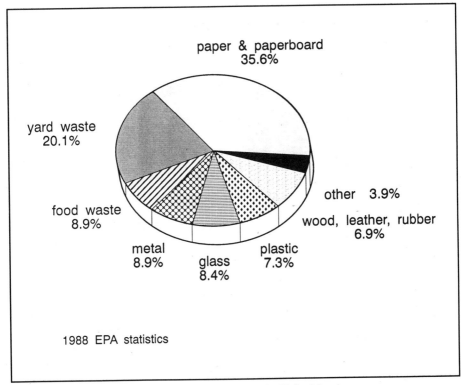

paper & paperboard
35.6%

yard waste
20.1%

food waste
8.9%

other   3.9%

wood, leather, rubber
6.9%

metal
8.9%

glass
8.4%

plastic
7.3%

1988 EPA statistics

Types of waste generated in the United States.

processing and manufacturing industries must be willing to use throwaways or scrap materials. And consumers must be willing to buy and use products made from recyclables. In other words, there must be a dependable demand for recyclables in both industrial and consumer markets.

The scrap processing industry, which has been involved for more than one hundred years in recycling metals, repeatedly emphasizes that collecting scrap materials is not the same as creating a demand for them. As industry spokespeople have said: "Scrap users, namely manufacturing industries, do not buy scrap materials simply because they are available. They must have a use for them, which is generated by demand for their finished products."

Demand, however, can be unpredictable, seesawing up then down again. That has been the case with paper recycling. Brokers, or collectors, who sell recyclable materials to processing companies, have been able to sell used newspapers for up to $75 per ton. But since 1984, "the amount of old newspaper collected has increased by 34 percent, glutting the market," according to a report in *Business Week*.[2]

There are not enough processors to recycle the huge volume of paper, and some collectors now receive only a few dollars per ton. In a number of states, collection centers have been forced to *pay* as much as $10 a ton to have the newsprint hauled away.

If collectors can find markets for old papers, they usually will not identify those who are buying. As the manager of a LaPorte, Indiana, recycling program noted recently: "We aren't talking about where we sell our waste paper. If we did (managers from) other programs and collection centers in northern Indiana would rush in, and we'd no longer have a market for our materials."

When there is little or no demand for old newspapers, some collection centers simply refuse to accept paper. Others may be able to afford the cost of storing huge bales of paper until a later date when they can find markets for newsprint. In most instances, though, newspapers become throwaways, adding to other paper materials that make up the major portion of solid waste in overburdened landfills.

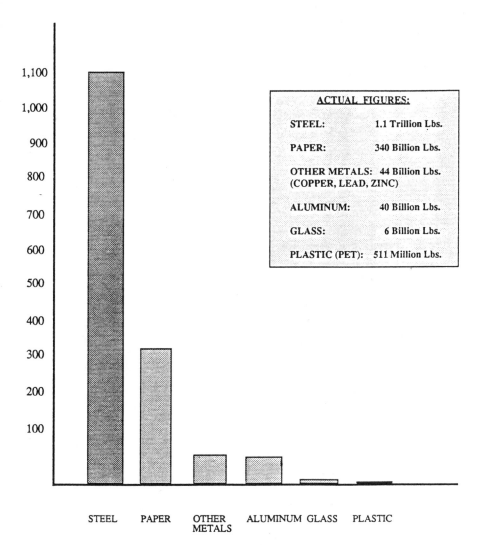

1,100					
1,000		**ACTUAL FIGURES:**			
900		STEEL:	1.1 Trillion Lbs.		
800		PAPER:	340 Billion Lbs.		
700		OTHER METALS: 44 Billion Lbs. (COPPER, LEAD, ZINC)			
600		ALUMINUM:	40 Billion Lbs.		
		GLASS:	6 Billion Lbs.		
		PLASTIC (PET):	511 Million Lbs.		

STEEL   PAPER   OTHER   ALUMINUM GLASS   PLASTIC
                  METALS

Measured in Billions of Pounds

(Glass and plastics figures are estimates.)

Comparative recycling rates, 10 years: 1979-1988

Because so many landfill sites are full and costs for new sites continue to increase, some states are talking about enacting laws that would require deposits on newspapers, similar to bottle and can deposits. Other suggestions include requiring publishers of newspapers and magazines to collect their old publications and dispose of them. Such schemes would put pressure on publishers to use more recycled paper, legislators say.

In an effort to increase demand for used paper, Connecticut recently passed a law that requires newspaper publishers who sell or print more than 40,000 copies of a newspaper within the state to use recycled paper in 20 percent of its sheets. By 1997, 90 percent of newspaper sheets must contain recycled fibers.[3]

Paper manufacturers also are under pressure to do something about the abundance of throwaway paper products. A few are adding processing equipment to their plants in order to manufacture recycled paper.

In spite of the paper glut, other recyclable materials, such as used glass bottles, aluminum cans, scrap iron and steel products, and some used plastics and fabrics, are still in demand. These recyclables are being collected in communities across the United States and in other industrialized nations.

Voluntary Recycling Programs

An increasing number of voluntary groups are involved in efforts to collect and separate throwaways and send them on to brokers or collection centers. Some of the programs have been started by youth groups, such as 4-H or the Boy Scouts and Girl Scouts, or civic organizations such as the Jaycees. Chapters of environmental organizations also help set up collection centers for recyclables.

A number of states—Alaska, California, Connecticut, New Jersey, Oregon, Washington, and Wisconsin, to name a few—have organized educational programs that explain the need for recycling. Some of the programs are geared for civic groups. but most are designed for school classroom use.

The Solid Waste Environmental Education Program (SWEEP) in California, for example, targets educational materials for elementary and middle school students. With filmstrips, posters, games, cartoons, and activity booklets, students learn conservation skills and ways in which solid waste problems can be overcome. Since the mid-1980s, thousands of California classes have been involved in SWEEP projects.

In the Portland, Oregon, school district, maintenance workers collect old textbooks, metals, glass, and polystyrene foam (a form of plastic) food trays. Then the materials are taken to the city's recycling

A recycling collection bin in Ventura, California.

center for processing. At the same time, students in more than fifty of Portland's public schools collect newsprint, cardboard, and white and colored school paper for recycling. Many classrooms have recycling boxes for paper, and in one school alone, the students collect enough paper materials to fill four fifty-gallon containers each week. "We don't have to wait until we are older and out of school to take some action to help protect our environment," said one middle-school student.

Collecting recyclables is not the only goal of school programs. Usually the purpose of a recycling curriculum is more broadly based, pointing up the importance of conserving and reusing the earth's resources and the variety of ways in which this can be done. Sometimes projects include hands-on experience, such as making paper from recycled materials.

To create awareness of how each individual contributes to the "garbage crisis," some students collect trash that they have generated over a week while in their classroom, cafeteria, shop, art room and gym. When the trash is dumped out on a classroom floor, it is dramatically apparent that garbage left to pile up would fill the room within a few weeks.

In some classrooms, students learn about composting, a form of recycling that creates ideal conditions for household wastes to decompose. A department of natural resources in some states provides guidelines for school classes that want to create mini compost piles—indoors in fish aquariums or outdoors in small fenced areas of schoolyards. Students can see biodegradable materials such as food scraps, leaves, grass clippings, and wood shavings break down in soil. The humus that remains can be used again by plants and animals.

Such an experiment is an opportunity to learn about other benefits of composting. Citizens can save on costs for plastic bags, and cities can cut back on their trash collection costs. According to the Wisconsin Department of Natural Resources, the state discards 2.4 million tons of compostable waste every year at a cost of between $65 and $75 a ton to collect and transport it to landfills.

In New Jersey, classroom activities on recycling point up how excess packaging materials—fancy boxes, plastic wraps, and so on—contribute to trash overload. Students conduct supervised experiments to show what happens to a variety of throwaways—from apple cores to cardboard to cans and glass—when they are burned. Students also study how a community determines where to place a trash disposal site, whether incinerator or landfill.

Even very young children can get involved in recycling efforts. In Connecticut, the Department of Environmental Protection has created a character called Ray Cycle ™, a superhero who is said to have come to life when a lightning bolt hit a garbage dump. In true superhero fashion, Ray "zooms" from school to school. Dressed in his yellow cape, green tights, and copper-colored boots, he uses songs and rap music to tell first, second and third graders about the need for waste reduction and recycling.

Mandated Recycling

"I think a pickup program like this should go on all over the city," said an elderly Chicago resident as he placed a blue plastic crate loaded with recyclables next to his garbage can on the street curb. That morning was the beginning of Chicago's experimental recycling program on the city's northwest side. One garbage truck came through the neighborhood picking up "regular" garbage. Another truck followed, with a worker picking up the bin filled with used glass bottles, plastics, and aluminum cans, sorting these materials and dumping the recyclables into large containers on the truck.

If the pilot program, which began in the fall of 1989, works well, officials plan a mandatory citywide program for sorting and collecting trash. Chicagoans can call the sanitation department's hotline to find out more about the program. "Ninety-five percent of the calls so far have been positive—people say they like the idea of recycling," said Feliberto Vega, a hotline operator.

Many other cities and towns in the Midwest are in the

experimental stages with recycling programs operated by municipal sanitation or waste management departments. But over the past few years, some states in the East and West have passed laws requiring communities to recycle and have set up facilities for collection. Rhode Island has been operating one of the largest recycling plants in the nation. The state facility collects and ships out more than 200 tons of recyclables each day to various processing centers.

In 1989, New York City passed a recycling ordinance that requires all households to separate their trash into three categories: (1) paper; (2) bottles, cans, and other recyclables; (3) all other refuse. Businesses and industries also are required to separate trash for recycling. Fines can be levied if trash is not sorted. In addition, a provision of the law requires that the city buy from suppliers who offer products made from recycled materials.

Recycling programs are in force in New Jersey communities. The Borough of High Bridge has had its program in place since 1987. Because of increasingly high charges for dumping garbage in landfills, the borough council decided that it could no longer afford waste disposal costs. Therefore, a program was designed to help pay for trash collection and disposal and also to encourage maximum recycling.

Municipal trucks pick up recyclable materials at curbside once a month at no charge. Or individuals and volunteer groups can take their recyclables to the Borough Garage, a collection center for aluminum cans, glass jars and bottles, and paper. But the borough charges a quarterly fee to pick up other garbage. Single family residences pay $35 every three months, and businesses and multifamily residences pay $50 per quarter.

Each building unit or household receives a year's supply of colored stickers—one for each week in the year. A sticker must be placed on every garbage bag or other container set out for collection. If additional stickers are needed, the cost is $1.25 apiece for single family residences and $1.65 for multifamily residences.

How are people accepting the program? Fairly well, according to High Bridge officials. Most residents have followed the regulations, and the amount of garbage the borough must haul has dropped about 30 percent. There has also been a dramatic increase in the volume of recyclable materials that High Bridge has been able to transport and sell to processors.

On the West Coast, Seattle, Washington, has initiated two successful recycling programs. A few years ago, the city council investigated the possibility of building a huge incinerator to burn its solid waste and convert it to fuel or electrical power, a "waste-to-energy" system as it is often called. But citizen groups were opposed to the incinerator because it could be a source of toxic air pollutants and would create problems in regard to disposal of the ash from burning. Moreover, the state had set waste reduction and recycling as top priorities for managing solid waste. Using mass burning to dispose of waste would discourage recycling, civic groups said, and city officials finally agreed.

Today, residents pay a monthly fee from city trucks to pick up two cans of refuse each week. But if people separate their recyclables from other garbage and fill only one trash container, their pickup charges drop $5.00 per month.

A local recycling company called Rabanco collects recyclable materials on the south side of Seattle. Another company, Recycle America run by Waste Management, Inc., the world's largest waste handler, picks up recyclables in the northern part of the city. With these two programs and individual collection efforts, the city now recycles about 30 percent of its solid wastes and hopes to double that within the next few years.[4]

By recycling half the newspapers Americans throw out annually,
the United States could reduce its waste by six million tons.

3

Recycling Paper, Glass, and Cans

If you have ever taken part in a recycling project or are involved regularly in efforts to recycle, you know that the most common materials collected are paper, glass, and cans. After these recyclables reach a collection center, they must be prepared for shipment to a processor or manufacturer who will use them as raw materials for new products.

Sources of Waste Paper

Americans collect about 30 percent of the total amount of waste paper generated each year—almost 26 million tons. According to the American Paper Institute (API), about 20 million tons of wastepaper goes to U.S. recycling mills to make new paper products. Six million tons are exported as raw materials for recycling mills in other countries.

Where is all the wastepaper coming from? Newspapers are one

familiar source. Perhaps you are one of the 50 million Americans who have been involved in community efforts to collect newspapers for recycling.

Offices are another major source of waste paper. In Portland, Oregon, office workers have voluntarily set up waste paper collection programs through a firm known as Wastech or through We-Cycle Office Wastepaper (WOW) operated by Weyerhaeuser, a major paper mill in suburban Beaverton. Both Wastech and WOW provide training on how to collect everything from computer printouts to junk mail. They also coordinate pickup by waste disposal companies.

The Port Authority of New York and New Jersey, whose buildings house hundreds of offices for private companies and government agencies, began a waste paper recycling program in 1974 with just a few offices. Today more than 300 collection centers for wastepaper have been set up in the Port Authority buildings. Part of the daily routine for most of the 10,000 employees is to deposit recyclable waste paper in the collection bins. Employees try to keep out contaminating materials such as carbon paper, film, glue, fasteners, waxed paper, and colored papers made with dyes. Even visitors and people who are just passing through the buildings deposit old newspapers in lobby bins. Income from the sale of the wastepaper pays for the costs of operating the program.

A number of supermarket chains, department stores, and factories throughout the United States also conduct on-going programs, collecting and baling corrugated (cardboard) boxes for recycling. Not only do those firms cover their operating costs but they also make a profit, sometimes totaling millions of dollars. More then 9 million tons of used corrugated boxes are recycled annually.

From Pulp to Paper

What happens to waste paper after it is taken to a collection or recycling center? If it has not already been sorted, the paper must be separated into newsprint, corrugated products, and office papers. Each kind of paper may be baled and then shipped by truck or rail to recycling mills. There the process of making paper uses basic techniques that are thousands of years old.

Although ancient peoples used a variety of materials to write on—silk, bamboo strips, and papyrus, for example—paper as we know it was first produced in China about A.D. 105. Papermakers shredded the bark of mulberry trees and mixed it with scraps of cloth. Then they soaked the mixture in water and pounded it into a pulp with a wooden mallet. The Chinese used a rectangular mold, probably made by stretching cloth across a bamboo frame, which they dipped into the pulp mixture. The thin layer of pulp on the mold dried in the sun, then was stripped off for use. Later the Chinese began making paper from old pieces of cloth and fishnet that they pounded into pulp.

Papermaking began in America 300 years ago as a recycling industry. Until 1860, paper was made primarily from cloth fibers—linen and cotton rags—as well as some wastepaper. With the increasing demand for paper over the next century and with new technology for using wood fibers, most mills phased out their use of rags. A few mills, however, use cotton clippings from textile plants to make high-quality paper for writing and printing.

Of the 600 or more paper mills in the United States, only about 200 use wastepaper exclusively, while 300 use from 10 to 50 percent wastepaper as raw materials. The remaining mills use lumber. Trees for papermaking are cut and the logs stripped of bark. Then the logs are cut into small chips, which are soaked and cooked with chemicals or ground to a pulp. Usually the pulp is further refined by adding chlorine bleach and heating again in a bleaching tower. The pulp mass is spread on a screenlike belt, pressed, dried and usually finished with a glossy coating made of clay. Then it is wound on rolls. Rolled paper is cut into smaller rolls or sheets for sale to fabricators.

Environmental groups have been highly critical of wood-pulp mills in recent years because such papermaking depletes vast forests. For example, if all copies of one Sunday edition of *The New York Times* could be recycled, about 75,000 trees would still be standing, the

Worldwatch Institute has estimated. Although trees are a renewable resource, they take years to grow. Cutting down forests also destroys "sinks," or holding places, for carbon dioxide (CO_2), which is one of the gases responsible for global warming and depletion of the ozone layer in the stratosphere.

As wood pulp is bleached and heated, chlorine combines with phenol compounds from wood, forming dioxins. EPA scientists and other researchers say dioxins in mill wastes have contaminated waterways and have been emitted into the air. Dioxin also has been found in paper products such as disposable diapers, coffee filters, and milk cartons.

Yet to date, the EPA has taken no regulatory action. Instead, more studies are being done to determine the levels of dioxin in wood pulp. Some European nations, on the other hand, have decided that bleached paper products pose dangers to human health and have banned some products made from bleached paper. Recycled paper products are being marketed instead.[1]

At a wastepaper recycling mill, the process of making paper is somewhat different from that used to process wood pulp. Recycling mills use wastepaper as raw material. The paper is dumped into a machine called a hydrapulper, which is rather like a huge kitchen blender, and mixed with water to form a slurry. Wastepaper slurry passes over screens that filter out nonfibrous materials such as glass, metal, plastic, and dirt. Layers of pulp on the screen have to be drained of excess water. Then the sheets pass between steam-heated rollers that dry and sterilize them, and the paper is smoothed and finished.

From a recycling mill, paper goes to fabricators who make newsprint, writing and printing paper, brown paper sacks, toilet and facial tissues, paper towels and napkins, and paperboard used to package a variety of products. Fabricators also use recycled paper pulp to produce insulation materials, molded packaging products such as egg cartons and flower pots, and shredded material to protect objects that might be damaged when transported.

Still, the demand for recycled paper helps determine how much

27

will be produced. If the demand increases, manufacturers will spend the money for equipment to recycle wastepaper or to build new recycling mills. In some cases, demand can be created through advertising and marketing programs. Consumers concerned about environmental problems often buy products that suggest a manufacturer is recycling or using natural resources wisely. The American Paper Institute encourages manufacturers to use recycled packaging materials for their products and to print the recycling symbol on their packages.

Glass: 100 Percent Recyclable

Toss out a glass jar or bottle and it is likely to be around for a million years. But a glass container does not have to be "buried alive" in a landfill or left as litter. In fact, at least ten states—Oregon and New York among them—require that consumers pay a deposit on glass bottles so that these containers will be returned to stores or collection centers for reuse or recycling.

Glass recycling follows fairly basic steps. Most collection centers

Products like these are packaged in recyclable paperboard; usually the recycled symbol appears on the box or carton.

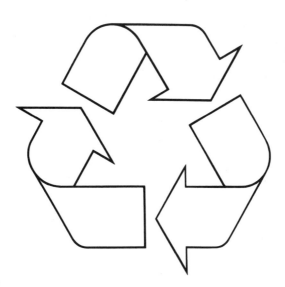

Companies that package their products in recycled paperboard use the recycling symbol to indicate that the carton is *made* from recycled paper. Companies producing paper products that *are* recyclable use the reverse of this symbol.

accept only glass that has been sorted by color—clear, amber (brown), and green. Metal caps and rings have to be removed, although paper labels usually can stay on the containers. From the collection center, used glass containers are shipped to a glass plant, where machines crush bottles and jars into small pieces called cullet. After the cullet is cleaned, other machines mix it with sand, soda ash, and limestone and then feed the mixture into a very hot furnace. Molten (melted) glass drops into molds and compressed air blows the glass against the walls of the mold, forming its shape. Newly formed bottles or jars are reheated and then cooled slowly, a process that prevents shattering.

After new glass bottles and jars are used, they can once again be recycled—over and over. In fact, glass is 100 percent recyclable. "This means that every pound of glass bottles and jars brought to a recycling center can make a pound of new glass containers," the Glass Container Industry says.

Aluminum Can Harvests

The average household in the United States discards 850 steel cans and 500 aluminum cans every year. Multiply that by the number of households in the nation, and the discarded cans total in the billions. But the good news is that an estimated two million Americans have become modern-day gleaners. In times past, gleaners picked up grain left in fields after the harvest. Today's gleaners harvest empty cans for a profit.

Aluminum cans are among the most profitable materials for collectors to recycle. Who are the collectors? Many are individuals—perhaps you are among them—who simply save used aluminum soft drink and beer cans and take them to collection centers or scrap metal yards and sell them. With mandatory recycling programs in some cities, many households set out aluminum cans for curbside pickup by municipal waste haulers. School groups, civic and religious organizations, job training centers for the handicapped, the poor and homeless, government workers, and employees of a variety of firms collect cans for recycling and for the income the cans bring.

In 1989, Americans collected about 45 billion aluminum cans, selling them to recycling centers for a total $900 million. Civic groups often use their earnings from cans to pay for special needs. For example, since 1985 firefighters across the United States have collected and sold enough aluminum cans to contribute over $1 million to buy equipment and supplies for children who are burn victims. One school in Utah used funds from its can recycling program to buy a public address system for its football stadium, while students in New Hampshire bought computers with recycling funds. Neighborhood associations from Alabama to Wisconsin have raised money through aluminum can recycling programs to improve their local parks. Zoos, animal care clinics, and humane shelters have benefited from can recycling programs.

Alcoa, a major aluminum manufacturer, has established a subsidiary known as Alcoa Recycling Company, which helps groups and communities across the nation set up aluminum can recycling programs. The company provides a packet of free materials that includes a guide for equipping and publicizing an aluminum can recycling effort.

Turning cans into cash motivates most people who recycle aluminum cans. But a survey by Alcoa showed that at least 24 percent of the can collectors interviewed wanted to take some action that would improve their environment.

The most obvious benefit of aluminum recycling is pulling cans from the solid waste stream and easing the load on landfills. Recycling also saves energy. Aluminum is made from bauxite ore, and 7.5 kilowatt hours of electricity are needed to produce each pound of metal from the ore. But 95 percent of that electricity is saved when aluminum is melted down and recycled.[2]

Boy scouts recycling at National Jamboree, Fort A.P. Hill, Virginia.

Recycling Food Cans

Steel cans also are part of the trash heap in most areas of the world. The tin-plated steel can has been used since 1820 to store and preserve foods and beverages. In the past, all steel cans were welded together, so liquids sometimes leaked from the seams. Steel cans were also heavy and tended to give drinks a metallic taste. Thus when seamless, light-weight aluminum beverage cans were first produced in the 1960s, they became the primary packaging choice for beverage companies. About 95 percent of all beverage cans ever produced in the United States have been aluminum.

Six hundred million pounds of used cans (about 22 billion cans) were recycled by Alcoa from the United States in 1989. Cans are purchased from consumers, shipped by rail from regional processing plants like this one, and sent to reclamation mills where the cans are remelted and rolled into sheet thin enough for a beverage can.

But steelmakers are now producing thin sheets of steel with even thinner coatings of tin that can be formed into seamless cans. Some beverage can makers have switched to steel because steel is less expensive than aluminum.

Food products, however, are still packed for the most part in regular (seamed) steel cans. And used steel containers of all types, like other throwaways, are part of the solid waste stream. Yet steel cans are being recycled, and the steel industry, long involved in the reuse of scrap metals, is actively seeking new ways to inform the public about steel can recycling through its Steel Can Recycling Institute formed in 1988. The institute began an aggressive campaign to add steel cans to the more than 100 billion pounds of scrap steel recycled each year in the United States.[3]

In the United States, scrap processors prepare eight million
tons of unwanted automobiles for recycling each year.

4

Scrap Isn't Junk

It's spring in Chicago, Illinois. In every neighborhood of the city, people are cleaning out garages, basements, sheds, and other storage areas. They haul broken bicycles, toys, and tools, worn-out stoves and refrigerators, rusty bed springs and countless other items to the street curbs or alleys. City workers will come along soon—as they do every spring during Clean-Up Week—to take the debris away in trucks.

What would happen, though, if discarded metal goods from households and waste metal materials from industry and businesses were simply left to pile up for months? In just one small factory that manufactures metal products, trim from stamping machines can fill up collection bins in a matter of hours. Within a year, the bins will fill up hundreds of times. Multiply that by thousands of factories that generate scrap metal materials. Then add scrap from bridges and buildings that have been torn down and from thousands of junk cars left on streets, alleys, or vacant lots each year. Because Chicago is a major transportation center, miles of old railroad tracks, discarded rail cars, and airplane parts increase the size of the scrap heap.

As you can imagine, if the scrap metals generated in Chicago each year were not picked up and recycled, most activities would stop. Health hazards would threaten every resident, and the city probably would become a ghost town. Or it might not even be visible since—*in one year*—there would be a mountain of scrap sixty feet high and ten square miles wide.

A History of Recycling

Fortunately, the scenario just described is not likely to occur since scrap metal is regularly picked up in cities across the nation and processed for reuse. In fact, throughout history, wherever and whenever scrap metals have been generated, they have been recycled.

Scrap metal recycling is an ancient practice. In times of war, farmers in ages past often converted their plows and other tools into swords and spears. Conquering armies tore down metal statues and ornaments, melting them down to form armor, weapons, household items, or other objects.

Throughout Europe, scrap iron dealers have collected and processed scrap iron and other metals for many centuries. During America's revolution, the colonists collected their copper and iron pots and metal utensils, depositing them in the town square. The metal goods were melted down to make weapons.

In the more recent past, scrap metal recycling was an important part of the industrial revolution. Immigrant peddlers of the late 1800s and early 1900s earned a living by collecting rags and old iron in horse-drawn wagons. Their cries echoed in the streets of eastern cities: "Rags-a-lion?" they called, running their words together in a chant. "Any rags-a-lion today?"

Many of these peddlers began scrap metal yards, collecting large amounts of scrap and processing it for resale and reuse in mills. Simon Krulewitch was an example. He came to the United States from Poland in the mid-1800s and began his scrap metal business in Chicago. After a major fire in 1871 leveled much of the city, Krulewitch was able to salvage iron fencing, pipes, gutters, and other metal materials from burned-out buildings. Eventually, profits from his peddling allowed him to open a large scrap yard that was a family business for three generations.

Many other family-owned scrap yards began operations in the late 1800s. These early scrap processors usually had only hand tools, such as sledgehammers and chisels, to help them break up large metal objects. It was hard, dirty, unglamorous work. Even after the turn of the century when huge machines became available, only a few scrap processors could afford to make a large capital investment in crushers, shredders, and balers. If scrap dealers spent large sums of money for expensive machinery, they had to recover their costs from sales of scrap materials or go out of business quickly.

Still, as more and more large scrap yards with modern equipment opened up, smaller family firms kept operating, too. Both the family and national companies were vital in providing the raw materials needed to produce military equipment during World War II.

TV star Ed Asner recalled working in his father's Midwest scrap yard during the war years. Asner told a Scripps Howard reporter that his father's yard, Asner Iron and Metal, was small and not equipped with "fancy machinery. We loaded and unloaded iron, cast iron, tin, galvanized metal, brass, copper . . . " by hand, Asner said. "We farmed out the heavy stuff, but I can remember my brother taking a hammer and chisel to some big cast-iron thing. It would take us weeks to chisel our way through."[1]

A Factory Without a Roof

Most family-owned scrap yards today have machinery to process "the heavy stuff." In fact, a scrap yard dealer, whether the owner of a small business or part of a huge national or international company, runs a factory without a roof, a place where raw materials are processed. You can find a scrap metal yard in or on the outskirts of almost every city in the United States.

When scrap metals come into a scrap yard, they must be sorted first into ferrous metals, or scrap that contains iron and steel, nonferrous materials such as aluminum, copper, and lead, and precious metals (gold and silver).

Ferrous scrap is by far the largest amount of material processed by a scrap yard, and it comes in the form of obsolete scrap—the type picked up from Chicago households during Clean-Up Week. Another major source of ferrous scrap is manufacturing plants that generate leftover materials, such as the scrap that comes from holes drilled into steel sheets to make auto parts. Steel mills also create scrap after forming raw steel into bars, sheets, and other shapes. All three categories of scrap materials must be further sorted into dozens of different grades and sizes that steel mills and foundries will use once again.

Huge machines in scrap yards slice, smash, pound, shred, and bale everything from automobile hulks to steel girders from buildings. If a

This mound of scrap metal must next be sorted into its many components.

car ends up in a scrap yard, tires, seats, window glass, battery, radiator, and most other parts would be removed. A crane then picks up the hulk and drops it into the bin of a hydraulic press, or baler. With thousands of pounds of pressure, the baler squeezes the car hulk into a compact bundle about the size of a large TV set.

In some scrap yards, car hulks are shredded on a huge machine that looks somewhat like a roller coaster. A crane picks up one carcass at a time from a mountain of car hulks in the yard. As each one is dropped onto the shredder, it is ripped apart in seconds. Steel hammers break through the shell somewhat the way a comb rakes through a thick head of hair. The fist-sized pieces then pass over magnetic drums that separate iron and steel from other metals and nonmetallic materials such as glass and plastic. The shredded pieces pile up on the ground at the end of a chute and eventually are loaded onto a freight car or truck—ready for shipment to a steel mill.

Scrap steel is now essential in steel manufacturing. In the past, nearly all steelmaking required virgin iron ore mined and shipped to mills, where it was melted down with coal, limestone, and scrap metals in basic oxygen furnaces. But more modern electric arc furnaces use nearly 100 percent scrap steel. Thus, every ton of new steel made from scrap conserves 2,500 pounds of iron ore, 1,000 pounds of coal, and 40 pounds of limestone.

Along with scrap steel, iron is processed and shipped to foundries, where it is recycled into cast iron products such as stoves, fences, and bells. From 1979 to 1988, 1.1 trillion pounds of ferrous scrap was recycled, more than double the amount of all other recycled materials combined.[2]

Metal Mines Above Ground

Of the nonferrous scrap collected, aluminum is a major recyclable. Scrap yards, like recycling collection centers, usually process aluminum beverage cans. Discarded aluminum lawn chair frames, siding and gutters from buildings, and aluminum scrap from industries such as mobile home and travel trailer manufacturers also are processed in a scrap yard. In all, nearly 3 million tons of aluminum scrap are prepared for reuse each year. Aluminum must be crushed and bundled or shredded before it can be shipped to a smelting plant, where it will be melted down to produce new aluminum.

Other metals recovered include lead—about 900,000 tons annually, primarily from car radiators—and 1.8 million tons of scrap copper. Nickel comes from stainless steel kitchen appliances and silver from used photographic film.[3]

"Is there gold in them thar' hills" of scrap? The question is a common one, and the answer is "Sometimes." Seldom would gold jewelry or gold coins be found in a scrap yard, but gold can be recovered from various industrial products. Gold is an excellent conductor of electricity, and the metal has been used in computer circuits, telephone systems, and even in high-quality spark plugs. Recovering gold from industrial wastes requires special equipment to flush the precious metal from other materials.

Through the efforts of scrap processors, countless throwaways enter the recycling loop and are reused. With all of the metals processed in the scrap industry, it is not surprising that scrap yards sometimes are called "metal mines above ground."

Barriers to Scrap Recycling

The scrap industry long has struggled with a variety of complex economic and environmental issues. In some cases, it may cost a steel mill less to use virgin raw materials than to buy scrap, particularly if the steel mill owns and operates iron ore mines. Scrap processors also may have to pay higher rates for transporting scrap metals than mining companies pay to ship ore, coal, and limestone.

In addition, like most other recyclers, scrap metal dealers cannot set their own prices for the goods they sell. Instead, mills and foundries that buy scrap metals determine what they will pay for the materials they need. At one time, a mill might pay $100 a ton for scrap and a

Aluminum wheels = Outdoor furniture

Stainless steel exhaust = Rail or subway car

Lead from auto battery = Flashlight batteries

Steel auto body = Household appliances

Copper cables = Telecommunications wiring

Many scrap products can be recycled, as is shown on this chart. When no longer useful, the items on the left can be recycled into the items on the right.

year or two later offer only half that amount. Then if there is little scrap available, a mill might pay well over $100 a ton for scrap.

Scrap processors either supply the scrap at the offered price or wait until the price rises. Since scrap processors must pay for the costs of preparing materials for recycling and transporting their goods to markets, they have to determine whether their income will exceed their expenses. In other words, they must make a profit in order to stay in business.

In recent years, the scrap metal industry has been faced with a dilemma in regard to manufactured goods that contain hazardous materials. Some examples are household appliances and fluorescent light fixtures that were once manufactured with electrical capacitors containing polychlorinated biphenyls (PCBs), a highly toxic chemical compound in the capacitor fluids. Although the Environmental Protection Agency banned PCBs in 1979, regulations did not cover PCBs in discarded appliances and other products. Then in 1988, the EPA determined that smashing and shredding products with PCBs leaves a contaminated residue. As a result, the EPA ruled that if the residue contains more than 50 parts per million of PCBs, it must be buried in a special hazardous waste landfill or incinerated. At the same time, however, intact appliances or capacitors with PCBs can be buried in regular landfills.

The new regulation meant that scrap processors had to pay the costs of transporting and disposing of the residue with PCBs. But processors could not earn enough from the sale of cut-up scrap appliances to pay the increased handling costs, so many scrap yards have refused to accept old refrigerators, air conditioners, and other products made with PCBs.

That situation, in turn, creates a ripple effect. Appliance dealers often have trouble selling new products when they cannot help their customers get rid of old ones. If sales fall, dealers may be forced to go out of business, which means losses to manufacturers.

Another environmental problem concerns air bags in automobiles. The U.S. Department of Transportation urged manufacturers to install air bags as safety features—they are designed to inflate on impact, protecting drivers if their cars crash. Sodium azide causes the bags to inflate, but if the chemical is unspent, it can be a health hazard. Not only is sodium azide highly toxic and a suspected carcinogen (cancer-causing agent), but it is also explosive. Yet no federal agency or auto manufacturer has made provisions for what to do with unused canisters of sodium azide when automobiles are discarded in scrap yards.

The Institute of Scrap Recycling Industries, which includes more than 1,800 companies, has attempted to point up the dangers of manufacturing goods without regard to their afterlife. In other words, the institute hopes that more and more manufacturers will reduce or eliminate their use of hazardous materials. As the institute points out: "It has been done before. When early electrical wiring caused household fires, new standards were put into place for the manufacture of safe electrical wiring and products. The use of [toxic] lead-based paints has virtually disappeared. Leaded fuel, while it can still be purchased, has declined markedly in its volume."

As has happened in the past, consumers must create a demand for products that will not harm the environment or human health. At the same time, scrap processors would like to see a national policy that promotes the design and manufacture of goods that can be recycled safely and efficiently.[4]

*Incinerators in the United States burn about 154,000
tons of waste every day, turning it into energy.*

5
—
Putting Waste to Work

Paper, glass, aluminum, scrap iron and steel—they are all recyclable.
But what about food and yard wastes, tires, and used motor oil? These
types of waste seem to have little in common, but all are being put to
work to produce energy. They also are being recycled for other
purposes.

Waste-to-Energy Debate

In the early 1980s, Portsmouth, New Hampshire, began burning trash
to generate steam that produced electricity, which was sold to a nearby
military facility. Converting waste to energy was a way for Portsmouth
to produce income at a time when federal aid to local and state
governments had been cut drastically. News articles called
Portsmouth's waste-burning effort "an unusual way to ease the budget
strain."

Today, cities as well as private businesses across the United States
have developed waste-to-energy plants not only to generate cash but
also to deal with the garbage disposal crisis. Some municipal

incinerators burn all solid waste without sorting or processing, producing energy in the form of steam that is recovered in a boiler. The steam may be used for industrial purposes, for heating buildings, or for generating electricity.

Although cities often burned solid waste in the past, most municipal incinerators were shut down after the 1970 Clean Air Act (and later amendments) banned hazardous pollutants emitted from smokestacks. Emissions from waste burners have polluted the air with sulfur dioxide (SO_2), nitrogen oxides (NO_x), and other gases that build up in the atmosphere, trapping heat from the earth, which in turn increases global temperatures, creating the greenhouse effect. The result could be a global warming that would change climate patterns and landforms worldwide. SO_2 and NO_x also are responsible for acid deposition, or acid rain. In the atmosphere, the gases form acidic substances that fall to the earth in wet or dry form and cause damage to lakes, forests, and some monuments and other structures.

Another major concern about mass burning is that many incinerators have released heavy metals and dioxins into the atmosphere. Dioxin compounds, which include seventy-five different species, have been linked to such health problems as birth defects and disorders of the immune system that leave people vulnerable to disease. Some of the most hazardous of the dioxin compounds have been found in emissions from older waste burners and in the remaining ash.

But as more and more municipal landfills have closed, city officials have had to find ways to dispose of waste. About 120 cities across the nation have built new mass-burn facilities that turn waste into energy. More than forty other waste-to-energy plants are under construction, and several dozen are in the planning stages. According to one study sponsored by the renewable fuel industry, each ton of solid waste that is burned can produce the amount of electricity a typical residence uses in a month.

Manufacturers of new waste burners also argue that air pollution control devices in burners keep toxic emissions within legal limits, and high temperatures destroy waste without producing large volumes of toxic ash. Wheelabrator Technologies, one of the major manufacturers of mass-burners, constructed a plant for metropolitan Baltimore, Maryland, in 1985. The incinerator burns more than half of the metropolitan area's solid waste—2,250 tons a day—at temperatures of 2,800°F. According to a report in *The Washington Post*, the heat from the plant "fires three huge boilers that produce steam for downtown Baltimore's central heating system and powers a generator that produces up to 55 megawatts of electricity for Baltimore Gas and Electric Co." Everything, except for medical and nuclear waste and construction material, is burned, and scrap metals are removed from the ash and recycled.

James Wood, a managing director for Wheelabrator told a *Post* reporter that filters in the plant remove more than 99 percent of the pollutants that otherwise would go up the smokestack. The remaining ash "is treated so that lead, cadmium, and mercury are bound in a chemical matrix that prevents decomposition in a landfill. That ash is taken to a secure landfill, lined with plastic and covered daily, so it's chemically inert," Wood explained.[1]

Nevertheless, critics say that burning waste is not an efficient way to produce energy because of the high costs (hundreds of millions of dollars) of building the plants and installing filters and scrubbers to prevent toxic emissions. In addition, citizens in some communities are still concerned about pollutants and have organized protests to fight the building of new mass-burners or they have campaigned for strict regulations on operating the burners.

Communities also have refused to allow waste incinerator ash to be dumped in landfills. One widely publicized case involved a Philadelphia incinerator that produced 15,000 tons of toxic ash. Since there was no place in Philadelphia or nearby areas to dump it, the ash was loaded on a barge called the *Khian Sea* for transport to an out-of-state landfill site.

The *Khian Sea* began its trip in late 1986. But like the barge load of Islip garbage, no one wanted the incinerator waste. No port along the Atlantic Coast would allow the *Khian Sea* to unload. The barge traveled to at least eleven other nations, where officials also refused the cargo, although the captain has been accused of dumping 2,000 tons of ash on a Haitian beach, causing environmental hazards. Finally, twenty-seven months later, in November 1988, the ash was dumped into the Indian Ocean. No one knows what the effect on sea life will be.

An alternative type of waste-burning technology is to sort materials that will burn from those that are noncombustible. Noncombustibles go to a landfill, and combustible materials are sorted into heavy and light components. The lighter materials are burned as a fuel (known as refuse-derived fuel) to produce energy. Heavier wastes are sorted further to remove glass and metals, then the remaining materials are mixed with wet sludge from sewage treatment plants. The mixture goes to a digester, where it decomposes, becoming humus, which is like compost, and is used to fertilize gardens and lawns.

Compost From Waste

Another method for dealing with solid waste is composting—the process of creating a pile of organic wastes such as food scraps, leaves, and grass clippings, layering these materials, adding moisture, and aerating (turning regularly to provide oxygen). Successful composting depends on adequate levels of moisture, oxygen, bacteria, and heat, all of which help organic materials decay. The end product can be used to fertilize or to help soil retain moisture.

Some midwestern and eastern cities have set up large composting sites for leaves. In the fall, leaves can represent about 20 to 30 percent of the solid waste collected and dumped at landfills. Huge leaf-loading machines sweep up leaves that have been raked or blown to the curb. The machines dump the leaves in heaps at a land site called a staging area. Tractors break up the leaves, which are watered, then formed into six- or seven-foot high piles known as windrows.

Just before winter, the volume of the windrows usually has shrunk by at least one-half, and the leaves are turned. The windrows maintain enough heat through the winter to aid in the decay process. In the spring and summer, the windrows are turned again. By the end of the summer, all the windrows are pushed together, and the decay process continues until the following spring, when the resulting compost is ready to be used as fertilizer.

A few U.S. cities are developing municipal composting systems to process all or most of their food and yard wastes. In 1988, U.S. Waste Recovery Systems, a subsidiary of the U.S. Waste Group, the nation's largest waste management company, set up the first composting system that uses a bacterial enzyme to transform garbage into compost. Known as the BDX Process, the privately owned system was installed in Sumter County, Florida, and processes 200 tons of garbage a day.

Turning solid waste into usable compost is not a new technology. "It was first used in municipal waste treatment in 1951," Roy Nelson, chairman of the U.S. Waste Group explained. But the time was not right for composting then. "Open landfills were abundant, tipping (dumping) fees were minimal, and individual waste removal bills were small," he said, adding that "composting is a natural alternative today" because landfills are closing and tipping fees are increasing. In addition, there is "widespread community rejection of incineration." Nelson believes that the Sumter County system will become the model for future municipal waste management because it reduces the volume of garbage placed in the landfill, extending its life by twenty times; eliminates odors, rodents, and insects; and costs 40 to 60 percent less than other types of waste disposal.

How does the BDX Process work? Ordinary municipal waste is delivered to the facility, where all recyclables, including plastics, are removed for resale. The remaining waste is then shredded into small particles called "fluff," which are laid out in windrows seven feet high and twelve feet wide. An aeration tractor mixes in a bacterial enzyme that "eats away at the garbage at such an accelerated rate that it creates heat up to 170 degrees," said Perry Senn, president of the Sumter County disposal system. Within three to six weeks, the waste becomes compost, which is then further screened to remove inerts, or inactive materials, that are buried in a landfill. The compost is bagged and sold or used to fertilize public parks, roadway berms (shoulders), or golf courses.[2]

The Big Oil Spill

Oil, of course, is a natural resource and a major source of energy for industrialized nations. But seldom do people think of putting waste oil—used motor oil—to work. According to the American Petroleum Institute, about 1.2 billion gallons of motor oil are sold each year. Half that amount is burned up in engines, while the other 600 million gallons is removed from cars at oil-changing time. When workers at a service station, garage, or similar facility change the oil in vehicles, they are required by law to collect the oil and store it in barrels until a hauler picks it up for processing or rerefining.

However, "Nearly 66 percent of the used motor oil generated in the United States (about 350 million gallons) is produced by the do-it-yourself mechanic changing his or her own oil," says API. Most of that oil is either poured on the ground or over a dirt or gravel road, buried in a yard, dumped in a sewer drain, or put in trash disposal bags or cans.[3]

Enough used motor oil is thrown out every seventeen or eighteen days to equal the oil spill of the *Exxon Valdez*, the oil tanker that ran aground off the coast of Valdez, Alaska, in March 1989. The tanker spilled 11 million gallons of crude oil into Prince William Sound, causing great ecological damage.

Although improper motor oil disposal does not lead to the kind of disaster associated with a major tanker spill, dumped oil can create a variety of hazards. It may seep into groundwater supplies, contaminating drinking water. Motor oil in sewer systems can disrupt bacteria that break down sewage. Oil in streams and lakes can interfere with the oxygen level in water, destroying aquatic life. Toxic substances in used oil may accumulate in the tissues of plants and animals that people eat.

A U.S. House of Representatives committee has been studying ways to deal with used motor oil under the Resource Conservation and Recovery Act, the federal law that allows the EPA to control the transport and disposal of hazardous wastes. But the federal agency and representatives of API say that designating used motor oil as hazardous and imposing rigid controls would discourage recycling efforts.

Recycling Used Motor Oil

Much of the used oil generated by do-it-yourselfers can be recycled. But that is easier said than done. It may be difficult to find a safe place to dispose of used motor oil. Service station and garage managers may not want to accept used oil, fearing that it could be mixed with antifreeze, degreasing agents, pesticides, or other contaminants. Getting used oil to recyclers could be a problem also if prices paid for it are low or service stations have to pay recyclers to pick up the used oil, which is the case in some states.

Another major obstacle is the lack of public awareness of the environmental dangers involved in improper dumping of used oil. Nor is there widespread understanding of the fact that used motor oil can be rerefined or used to produce energy. As the petroleum industry has pointed out, if all the used oil generated each year could be burned to generate electricity, the energy needs of nearly 900,000 homes would be met. Most used motor oil, however, is reprocessed for use in the steel industry, in asphalt plants, and in other industries that burn fuel in kilns.[4]

Informing the public about the need for recycling used motor oil is then a primary task. Next comes the job of setting up statewide or local oil recycling programs. Some city governments have curbside pickups. Garbage haulers collect used oil that has been drained into disposable containers. Oil is stored until it can be sold to an oil rerefiner.

Volunteer programs have been established in some parts of the nation. The American Petroleum Institute has published a booklet describing a model program for recycling used motor oil. The booklet includes information on how to get sponsors for a program and set up recycling containers in service stations or garages. It also contains sample public service announcements, press releases, and thank you letters, and lists oil recycling coordinators in all of the states and the District of Columbia. Coordinators may work in a department of environmental protection, waste management, or natural resources, or

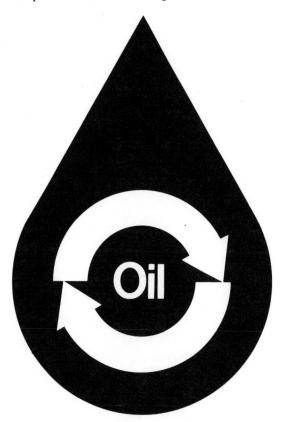

This symbol is used to remind people to recycle used motor oil.

in a similar agency. They provide technical information about the problems of used oil disposal.

240 Million Scrap Tires!

Of the 240 million tires discarded each year, about 27 percent are reused—recapped or turned into new rubber products. But the rest are dumped. Although some landfills accept scrap tires, most operators do not want that type of solid waste. Tires are designed to be nearly indestructible and do not compact well because of their air pockets. Unless scrap tires are buried carefully—deep underground and mixed well with other wastes—they will "float" or rise to the surface.

Tires that come to the surface of a landfill or tires stored above ground present another type of problem: the water that collects in them provides breeding sites for mosquitoes. Scrap tires above ground also may attract rodents that spread disease. In addition, tires are combustible, and if they pile up, they become fire hazards. Sometimes arsonists set fire to piles of tires, which may burn out of control, creating heavy smoke pollution.

Minnesota was one of the first states to set policies and pass legislation to deal with problems associated with discarded tires. The state banned used tires from landfills in 1985. If tire stockpiles are hazardous to public health, owners must clean up their sites. Minnesota provides financial help for the cleanup if the stockpiles were in existence before the 1985 law was passed.

What happens to the scrap tires? Minnesota waste management officials investigated a number of options for recycling tires, such as burying them in soil to prevent erosion and using them to fabricate products like floor mats, gaskets, dock bumpers, and fencing. But such applications consume only small quantities of the scrap tires. Larger volumes of them are ground to make a pulverized rubber known as crump rubber, which in turn is combined with binders to produce rubberized sealers and asphalt rubber for highways and athletic surfaces.

In a number of states, scrap tires are being put to work as fuel. As with other waste-to-energy facilities, tire-burning plants generate electricity. The California-based Oxford Energy Group, for example, has developed a variety of resource recovery systems across the nation, among them the first U.S. facility to produce energy from waste tires. The power plant is located in Modesto, California. Nearby, the landscape is covered with some 40 million discarded tires, the fuel source for the power plant. Approximately four or five million tires are added to the stockpile each year, providing enough fuel for energy needs over the next decade or more.

Several dozen resource recovery plants across the United States produce tire chips that can be used as fuel by paper and cement companies. Generally, in cement manufacturing, limestone and clay are heated in a high temperature kiln (furnace) and then ground with

Discarded tires like these, dumped in a rural area in Michigan, can attract pests and also be a fire hazard.

gypsum to produce cement. Although cement plants in Germany, Austria, and France have been using tire chips as fuel for cement-making since the mid-1970s, U.S. cement kilns usually use coal or natural gas as fuel. But at least two plants—Genstar Cement in Redding, California, and Arizona Portland near Tucson—burn tire chips. Kiln temperatures reach up to 2,800°F, which is hot enough for complete combustion of waste tires, including their steel belts and beads. As one expert explained: "What is so fantastic about firing rubber in large rotary kilns is the fact that all the ash, metal, and volatiles (synthetic organic compounds) are consumed in the cement—there is no waste."[5]

If compacted, the amount of plastics thrown out each year would fill 125,000 four-bedroom homes.

6

Problems With Plastics

From plastic bottles and cups to plastic telephones and toothbrushes, plastic goods—perhaps more than any other products—have become symbols of a society geared for convenience and consumption. The use of plastic also helps merchants and manufacturers sell large quantities of goods. In supermarkets and self-service stores, retailers and customers want products that are packaged and ready to take to the check-out counter. Unlike the past, when retail clerks selected the items that customers wanted, today's shoppers usually make their own choices from shelves and racks of goods. Plastic packaging protects many items from damage. Buy a camera, for example, and you will find it inside a box, nestled in a form-fitting mold probably made of polyurethane, or rigid foam plastic. Pick up a dozen eggs from the grocery store, and they could be packaged in polystyrene, the same kind of light foam plastic used for fast foods.

Fast-food restaurants depend on plastic packaging to sell convenience along with their products: plastic containers can be thrown out after use. Supermarkets sell convenience with their packaged products, too. How about those plastic squeeze bottles that are not only shatter-proof but also allow you to dispense catsup and mustard with ease and without much mess? Squeezable containers are made of several kinds of plastic, which gives the bottles their shape, flexibility, and strength.

There are frozen foods packaged in polyethylene terephthalate (PET) bags that can be boiled or microwaved right in their containers. PET is also the plastic used for two-liter beverage bottles. Plastic milk jugs are made of high-density polyethylene (HDPE). Polypropylene is a type of plastic used for bottles of syrup and shampoo; all of these plastic containers are break-resistant. A variety of plastic bread and produce bags made of low-density polyethylene (LDPE) keep foods fresh.

Many other common products are packaged in plastic—single doses of medications may be in "blister" packs of fairly rigid polyvinyl chloride (PVC). Cosmetics, household items, hardware, games, and toys come encased in a variety of plastic materials. And, of course, most purchases are placed in plastic bags for customers to carry from the store.

Explosion of Plastic Goods

Plastics were first produced during the early-1900s. But they developed rapidly during World War II, when they were used as substitutes for scarce materials, particularly metals. The versatility, light weight, and strength of plastic materials made them ideal for a variety of military purposes and later for consumer goods.

Today, plastics have become so much a part of our way of life that most people would have difficulty imagining life without them. According to the Center for Plastics Recycling Research at Rutgers University, more than 57 billion pounds of plastics were produced in 1987. The total is expected to increase to about 75 billion pounds by the year 2000, and a projected 38 billion pounds will be thrown away.

Whether used in products or packaging, plastic materials make up only 7.3 percent of the total U.S. waste in weight, but by volume they account for 20 to 30 percent of the total. Why? Because plastic products do not break down easily. A prime example are so-called disposable diapers, which are lined with plastic. They were first introduced in the 1960s, and since then people with infants and small children have been buying disposable diapers by the billions. The diapers pile up in landfills at the estimated rate of five million tons a year. Most will not disintegrate for hundreds of years.

The chemical characteristics that make plastic versatile and strong also prevent breakdown of the materials except by burning or by oxidation over long periods of time. Plastic is made from synthetic resins, which are produced from such natural resources as oil and coal. Each molecule of resin is made up of long chains of hydrogen and carbon atoms called polymers. The polymers are so tightly bound

Various plastic goods that do not biodegrade.

together that bacteria and fungi, which usually break down organic materials, cannot penetrate the chain. Thus, plastic materials are almost indestructible.

Because of their long life, plastic products are hazardous for many kinds of sea life. For example, sea lions, seabirds, and turtles become entangled in discarded plastic rings made to hold beverage cans, choking to death or starving because they cannot move. Or they mistake plastic bags or small pellets—waste from plastic manufacturing plants that have washed onto beaches—for food. When animals and birds swallow plastic materials, they may suffer internal injuries or a false feeling of fullness that makes them stop eating, thus starving themselves.

What to Do With All That Plastic?

There is no simple answer to that question. Burning could dramatically reduce the amount of plastic waste, but some federal agencies and environmental groups are concerned that incineration would create hazardous by-products. If plastics are burned in an incinerator at temperatures below 1,650°F, they can produce dioxins. There also are fears that ash from incinerated plastic, as well as with other types of waste burning, would contain dioxins and other toxic elements that would contaminate the soil and water if disposed of in landfills. However, the plastics industry cites tests by the Midwest Research Institute that show combustion temperatures as high as 2,800°F prevent the production of dioxin.

In some states, legislators want to enact outright bans on all plastic packaging or taxes that would deter the use of plastics. A few states already have laws on the books to prohibit certain plastic products. Nebraska, for example, has banned the sale of nonbiodegradable disposable diapers by 1993. Iowa, Oregon, and Washington are considering similar laws. Maine has banned the use of juice bottles made with layers of different types of plastic.

Cities, too, are passing antiplastic legislation. In St. Paul and

Minneapolis, ordinances decree that all food and beverage packaging must be "environmentally acceptable"—that is, degradable, recyclable, or returnable. Such products as plastic egg cartons and catsup bottles are banned.

On the other hand, plastic manufacturers point out that bans on plastic materials do not really solve the waste disposal problem. As Amoco Chemical has argued in a company statement: "A 1987 study in Germany showed that if plastic packaging was replaced entirely, the energy needed to produce the packaging would double, the weight of packaging would increase four-fold, the cost of packaging would more than double, and the volume of waste collected would increase about two and one-half times."

Producing degradable plastics is the most recent effort to deal with the problem of plastic wastes. One type of degradable plastic photodegrades, or breaks down, when exposed to the ultraviolet rays of the sun. Through a chemical process, light-sensitive molecules, called carbonyls, are added to plastic polymers, or light-sensitive chemicals are mixed with the plastic resin. In sunlight, the chemicals weaken the polymers, which break down and become shorter. Eventually the plastic breaks into small fragments and decomposes.

Biochemists also combine synthetic resins with natural polymers of cornstarch or cellulose and vegetable oil to make plastic biodegradable. Bacteria feed on the natural polymers, which promote their growth, then they "attack" plastic polymers that might not appeal to them otherwise.

Another type of biodegradable plastic is in the experimental stages. Researchers at James Madison University in Virginia are modifying the genetic structures of bacteria to create "biopolymers." The process begins with a bacterium, *Alcaligenes eutrophus (A. eutrophus)*, that manufactures a plastic-like polymer known as PHB, storing it in granules inside cell walls. The bacterium uses PHB when it needs energy.

According to a report in *Science*, biochemists can grow colonies of *A. eutrophus* in a glucose solution. The bacteria are "deprived of nitrogen, which the bacteria interpret as a sign that rough times are ahead. Much as bears add on an extra layer of fat before hibernation, the bacteria then devote most of their resources to making PHB." Polymers must then be recovered from the bacteria and the granules melted to form a plastic material similar to polypropylene. However, unlike polypropylene, the bacteria-produced plastic can be broken down by microorganisms.[1]

A number of degradable plastic products are already on the market, such as biodegradable bags and disposable diapers. A growing number of communities require the use of degradable grocery and waste disposal bags. In 1988, a federal law was passed that requires manufacturers to use photodegradable plastic to make six-pack rings, but plastic rings do not break down easily when they are discarded in the ocean or in lakes.

Although degradable plastics might eliminate some litter, they do not seem to be the answer to the problem of growing waste heaps in landfills. No matter what the structure of the plastic, it cannot break down in any short period of time when entombed in a landfill without sunlight and air. Secondly, if degradable plastics do decompose, there is the question of what happens to the shards of plastic that are left. Joan G. Harn, an analyst with the U.S. Office of Technology Assessment (OTA), which provides research reports for Congress, believes that the use of degradable plastics is a "questionable" way to deal with solid waste problems. She noted that scientists have not yet learned how the materials react when burned or buried in a landfill or recycled with nondegradable plastics. No one is sure whether toxic chemicals, such as benzene, styrene, ethylene, phenol, and propylene, which are used in the production of some plastics, will be released into the air, soil, and water.

Other arguments against degradable plastics come from established plastic manufacturers. An official of Dow Chemical, for example, has suggested that biodegradable plastic would be weaker and thus less reliable than plastics made of all synthetic resins. Plastic companies also believe that production of degradable plastics might convince the public that plastic recycling is not needed. Recycling is the type of action that plastic makers favor, as do some environmental groups.

What About Plastic Recycling?

To date, only about one percent of the plastic manufactured each year is recycled. Most plastic materials that are recycled are used to make products quite different from their original form. Sixteen-ounce soft-drink bottles made of PET are the most common recyclable containers. Manufacturers process PET bottles to make fibers ranging from carpet yarns to rope, fluffy fill for sleeping bags and pillows, and such products as scouring pads, fence posts, and parking space bumpers. HDPE containers (milk and water jugs) are turned into flowerpots, toys, pails, trash cans, speed control bumps, and a variety of synthetic lumber products such as outdoor furniture and playground structures. Used vinyl may be refabricated to make pipes and fittings, floor tile, truck bed liners, and insect traps.

In many cases, waste plastics that are collected are a mixture of different resins. Sorting the plastics can be very costly, so manufacturers have developed ways to use mixed plastics to make substitute lumber products for a variety of purposes.

Then there is polystyrene—plastic foam products such as the "clamshells" that hold sandwiches from fast-food restaurants. Plastic foam containers seem to pop up everywhere, littering landscapes and waterways. Some consumer groups and environmental organizations have been highly critical of the increasing use of polystyrene containers. Such products were once primarily made with chlorofluorocarbons (CFCs), one of the chemicals that contributes to depletion of the ozone, a layer of gases in the stratosphere that protects the earth from the sun's ultraviolet rays. But in 1988, manufacturers of plastic foams began to phase out their use of CFCs to make foam plastics, and the foam food packaging companies stopped using CFCs altogether.

Still, foam products fill up many trash bins and add to the landfill crunch (and calls for plastic bans). Because of that threat, the plastics industry began a major effort in 1989 to set up collection and recycling of polystyrene wastes. According to news reports, several manufacturers have contributed $2 million each to form the National Polystyrene Recycling Company (NPRC). The corporations involved are Amoco, Arco, Chevron, Dow, Huntsman Chemical, Mobil, Fina Oil, and Polysar. Through NPRC, they have established five regional polystyrene recycling plants. One of these facilities is Plastics Again in Massachusetts, which processes polystyrene food trays from school cafeterias. The trays are ground up and melted into pellets that will be used to make new products ranging from videocassette boxes to trash cans.[2]

Because plastics recycling is a fairly recent process, the Plastic Bottle Institute, which is a division of the Society of the Plastics Industry, has developed a coding system to indicate the types of resins used to make plastic containers. The coding system is designed to help recycling centers and about 170 companies that recycle plastics or make equipment for the recycling process.

A few states have adopted the codes for their recycling programs, but others oppose the symbols. Opponents say that using a symbol gives the impression that the container is made from one type of plastic. But, according to the coding system, the container can be made primarily of one plastic—HDPE, for example—and several other kinds of plastic resins as well.

Some companies that use foam food containers also are getting into the recycling act. The McDonald's Corporation is an example. Critics had been particularly vocal about the vast quantities of foam products used by the more than 10,000 McDonald's restaurants worldwide, even thought the company had switched to a foam packaging that is made without CFCs and is recyclable. In 1990, the company began recycling efforts in more than 450 of its restaurants in New England. In addition, McDonald's uses millions of dollars worth of recycled plastic building materials and recycled paper products.[3]

Criticism of McDonald's foam packaging continued, however, and in early 1991, the company began wrapping food in paper. Yet coated paper and paperboard used for foods are not, at present, easy to recycle and may end up in a landfill, too. And some studies show that more energy is used to manufacture paper products than to manufacture polystyrene. But McDonald's says it will continue its campaign to reduce its use of throwaway materials and reuse and recycle as much as possible.[4]

CODE	MATERIAL	% OF TOTAL BOTTLES
♳ 1 PETE	— — — — Poly-Ethylene Terephthalate (PET)*	20-30%
♴ 2 HDPE	— — — — High Density Polyethylene	50-60%
♵ 3 V	— — — — Vinyl / Polyvinyl Chloride (PVC)*	5-10%
♶ 4 LDPE	— — — — Low Density Polyethylene	5-10%
♷ 5 PP	— — — — Polypropylene	5-10%
♸ 6 PS	— — — —Polystyrene	5-10%
♹ 7 OTHER	— — — — All Other Resins and Layered Multi-Material	5-10%

These symbols are used to designate different types of recyclable plastic.

7

Managing Hazardous Wastes

A man in a suburban neighborhood lifts off a street sewer cover and pours in a bucket of oily goo. Construction workers toss bags of asbestos, a hazardous building material, in a field. Late at night two truckers dump corroded and leaking drums of toxic liquids under a bridge. Trash haulers decide not to make a long and expensive trip to an incinerator where hospital wastes are burned and instead illegally dump bags of needles, blood vials, and even body parts into a ditch.

The individual actions just cited are ways that some hazardous materials become threats to human health. Other threats come from huge amounts of toxic wastes once dumped in city landfills that have since been abandoned. Some present landfills not licensed for hazardous materials also illegally accept toxic wastes. In addition, agriculture, the military, power plants, manufacturing, mining, and many small businesses produce, use, or store hazardous materials that can be a danger to public health and the environment.

Hazardous Waste Sites

In the past, manufacturers routinely disposed of industrial by-products and leftovers by burying the materials near factories. Industrial waste also was used as fill for wetlands or low-lying areas that were converted to construction sites, or to fill in excavations left after buildings were torn down. Materials were expected to break down after being dumped on land, and it was commonly believed that soils would filter toxic chemicals before they washed into waterways or seeped into groundwater.

Now, however, many old dump sites for industrial wastes are "toxic time bombs." Americans became alarmed about such waste sites when they learned in 1978 about a dump near Niagara Falls, New York, called Love Canal. People living near the site developed mysterious ailments, and children were born with physical defects. Investigators soon learned that the abandoned canal once had been used as a dump site for toxic chemical wastes that had contaminated soil and drinking water, creating health hazards.

The discovery at Love Canal led to investigations of other dump sites across the United States. Within a few years, more than 1,000 waste disposal areas were labeled hazardous. At the end of 1980, Congress passed the Comprehensive Environmental Response, Compensation and Liability Act, which provided a "superfund" for cleaning up toxic waste sites. Since passage of the act, now known as Superfund, Congress has allocated about $10 billion through 1992 for the Superfund program, which the EPA oversees. However, Superfund requires that those responsible for toxic wastes pay a major portion of the costs for cleaning up the 275 million tons of hazardous materials generated each year.

The EPA has listed more than 1,200 waste disposal sites that are in need of priority cleanup. Most are in the northeastern and southeastern states, which generate about 200 million tons of hazardous waste each year. The sites may be old landfills, burial grounds for drums of toxic wastes from chemical plants, petroleum refiners, and other industries. More than 100 Superfund sites are federal facilities—military posts and nuclear weapons plants, which for years have used poor waste disposal practices. Toxic substances, including explosives, radioactive wastes, degreasers, and pesticides, leak from federal and private sites and contaminate rivers, streams, and groundwater.

According to a 1991 report from The National Toxics Campaign Fund, many more military installations have not been designated for priority cleanup but contain thousands of hazardous waste sites. The report lists 1,579 military installations with 14,401 sites contaminated with hazardous materials. It will cost up to $200 billion to clean up the military's toxic waste.[1]

Of the Superfund sites only a few dozen have been totally decontaminated. In many cases, toxic wastes in a landfill are simply contained. Like other wastes they are capped with clay. The area also is double-lined with vinyl or other synthetic material to prevent toxins from moving. Some wastes undergo chemical or biological treatment that can destroy toxic substances or prevent their movement through the ground. Or the soil with hazardous substances may be washed—drowned with water and the runoff collected and treated to remove toxins.

Although the EPA plans to close most land disposal sites for hazardous waste, some will be allowed to accept material. In such cases, the landfills must include a system to collect leachate so that it will not seep into groundwater.

The EPA also allows some hazardous waste to be burned at high temperatures in incinerators. But many environmental groups (including The National Toxics Campaign Fund) are protesting this method of disposal, because incinerators emit toxic fumes into the air.

To date, more than half of the Superfund money has been spent for studies, consultants, legal fees, and administration, according to a report from the OTA. The agency charges that "contractors keep busy, reports pile up, contamination spreads into soil and groundwater," while many sites wait for cleanup.

EPA Administrator William K. Reilly, former head of a national environmental group, agrees with much of the criticism, which comes not only from the OTA but from other government and civic organizations as well. Reilly has promised to cut back on consultants and hire new personnel to enforce hazardous waste regulations.

Who's Responsible? Who Pays?

Communities in almost every state are struggling to determine how to handle hazardous wastes and how to determine who should be responsible for cleanup costs. One ongoing dispute centers on the Lowry Landfill, a waste site southeast of Denver, Colorado, that was closed in 1980. According to a report in *The Denver Post*, 158 companies and government agencies, including the U.S. Mint and municipal sewage districts, dumped pollutants at Lowry for more than a decade. Among the major contributors were a dozen or more large manufacturing companies such as Coors, IBM, Hewlett-Packard, Honeywell, Storage Technology (a manufacturer of storage devices for computers), and several oil companies.

The EPA has identified 102 chemical pollutants and nine radioactive substances at Lowry Landfill, but the agency has not yet determined how much each landfill contributor will pay for cleanup work. At issue is a settlement that EPA made with Storage Technology when it went into bankruptcy, allowing the company to pay $5.9 million as its share of cleanup costs.

A coalition of former landfill customers believes the EPA settlement is unfair. They contend that Storage Technology, which has reorganized, shipped about one million gallons of toxic chemicals to Lowry Landfill, ranking as one of the top contributors in volume of hazardous wastes. The coalition believes that Storage Technology should be responsible for more than $70 million of the total cleanup costs, which could go as high as $4.5 billion. But a final decision on cleanup liability for Lowry Landfill has yet to be made.

Another case centers on the now defunct Avtex Fibers plant on the

Shenandoah River in Warren County, West Virginia. The rayon manufacturing plant, which once employed 3,000 workers, operated for nearly fifty years and was often cited for environmental problems. In 1988, state agencies sued Avtex for violating laws that limit emissions of carbon disulfide, a highly toxic and flammable solvent, and for dumping polychlorinated biphenyls (PCBs) into the Shenandoah. PCB compounds were once widely used as fire retardants and heat resistors, but because of their toxicity they have been banned in many products.

Avtex officials claimed that the company was making repairs to the plant as a means of cleaning up its pollutants, but the state and the EPA said Avtex made improvements only when forced to do so. The EPA fined the company $300,000 for continuing to discharge industrial waste into the river. As a result, the company abruptly shut down its fiber plant in November 1989, leaving behind 1,400 barrels of hazardous chemicals, polluted lagoons on the 400-acre site, and possible contamination of waterways. It is expected to take years for the courts to determine how much of the estimated $100 million in cleanup costs Avtex should pay.[2]

A Toxic Inventory

Although some industries are making efforts to clean up or reduce toxic wastes, manufacturing and processing plants across the nation still are sources for many toxic pollutants. Until recently, no one knew what kinds of substances factories released. Members of Congress became concerned about the problem after a 1984 leak of toxic chemicals from a Union Carbide plant in Bhopal, India. The chemical emissions killed 3,000 people and injured 50,000 more. In 1986, Congress enacted amendments to the Superfund act, giving the EPA authority to require industries to report the types of chemicals they use or discharge into the environment. Citizens also have the right to request information about chemical hazards in their communities. In addition, cities and towns are required to develop disaster plans to deal with chemical spills or leaks.

In mid-1989, the EPA announced that its inventory of toxic emissions from 19,278 factories (about 75 percent of those required to report) totaled over seven *billion* pounds. The EPA received reports on 328 toxic chemicals, some of them known or suspected carcinogens, in a wide range of industries, including chemical manufacturers, oil refiners, food processors, textile makers, and plastic and metal fabricators.

The largest amounts of toxic emissions came from refineries and chemical plants in Louisiana and Texas. An Alcoa plant in Point Comfort, Texas, topped the list of industries emitting toxic chemicals, releasing more than one million pounds of pollutants per year. However, a large percentage of Alcoa's chemical emissions are aluminum oxide, which company officials say is not harmful and the EPA plans to drop from its list of toxic substances.

Gerald Poje, a toxicologist with the National Wildlife Federation, opposes the EPA plan. He believes that aluminum oxide can be a health hazard and that no toxic substance should be dropped from the EPA's list without learning more about the effects of its toxicity on humans.

Scientists have been unable to determine the health effects of chemical pollutants because there are so many variables. Some relatively harmless chemicals may react with others to create health and environmental hazards. Others that are harmless in small amounts may accumulate over ten to twenty years in fatty tissues, leading to health problems. Air pollutants can travel long distances and may deposit on water or land, sometimes breaking down, other times building up or ingested by plants, animals, or fish and moving up the food chain to human consumption.[3]

There also are many uncertainties about how much industrial emissions contribute to the local amount of pollutants—particularly air pollutants. Other major sources are motor vehicles, power plants, and military facilities. But the EPA inventory helped prompt 1990 amendments to the Clean Air Act, which was first enacted in 1970.

The new amendments set tougher regulations for disposal and reduction of toxic waste from a variety of sources.

Hazardous Waste Controls

In efforts to get rid of toxic wastes, some communities are turning to waste haulers who specialize in hazardous waste disposal—a fast-growing and profitable business. Major haulers dump hazardous wastes in landfills they have set up under strict federal guidelines. But some firms ship waste across international borders. Shipments of hazardous materials from the United States have gone to such nations as Haiti, South Africa, Japan, Britain, Mexico, and Canada. Other industrialized nations, including Germany, Italy, Great Britain, and New Zealand, also export their toxic waste. Most of it goes to developing countries, where dumping costs are low and regulations to control pollutants barely exist.

Some receiving countries and environmental groups with international ties, such as Greenpeace, are protesting the practice, however. Caribbean and African nations have called for a complete ban on wastes from foreign sources. The United Nations Environmental Program has proposed an international treaty that would regulate and reduce the toxic waste shipments across international borders.

Within the United States, demands have increased for strict regulations to control hazardous waste disposal. The EPA announced that it would offer rewards of up to $10,000 to people who provide information leading to conviction of polluters. EPA's Criminal Enforcement Counsel (401 M Street, SW, Washington, D.C. 20460) is responsible for prosecuting offenders.

Yet controlling toxic waste requires much more than whistle-blowing. The EPA also has proposed stiff penalties for lawbreakers. In March 1989, for example, the EPA imposed a fine of $2.7 million on the Four County Landfill in Rochester, Indiana, for illegally accepting hazardous waste—the landfill was not designed for that purpose and lost the right to take in toxic materials. Several months later, EPA fined a Casmalia, California, landfill operator $6.2 million for taking in more toxic waste than it was authorized to handle. The agency also imposed a $15 million penalty against Texas Eastern Transmission Corporation, a natural gas pipeline company, because PCBs contaminated soil along the company's 10,000-mile pipeline from Texas to New Jersey.

The Federal Bureau of Investigation (FBI) has been working with the EPA since 1982 to investigate illegal transport, storage, and disposal of hazardous wastes. FBI Director William Sessions noted that some waste haulers and industries have illegally dumped toxic materials rather than dispose of them in a safe (and more costly) manner. Federal laws that took effect in May 1990 ban disposal of any chemicals that have not been treated. Sessions has warned that people who deliberately pollute for profit or through carelessness would be prosecuted. He told a United Press International (UPI) reporter that tough criminal laws against polluters would "force companies and individuals to install and to maintain sound protection systems."[4]

At the state level, some legislatures have passed waste disposal laws that are more stringent than federal controls. This policy is particularly true regarding laws to combat careless disposal of medical waste. The laws were prompted by well-publicized incidents of medical debris that included bloody bandages and used syringes washing up on seacoast beaches during the summers of 1987 and 1988. Within that same period, children in Indianapolis, Indiana, found discarded blood vials in an unlocked dumpster behind a medical clinic and playfully smashed the vials against a wall. One of the vials contained blood from a victim of AIDS. In another incident, Ohio children found medical syringes in an open dumpster and jabbed each other with the needles as they played doctor.

Rubbish from hospitals and clinics does not fall under federal hazardous waste regulations, although Congress is considering national guidelines. But about half the states have adopted new laws or revised old regulations to toughen requirements for the treatment

Syringes and blood vials are examples of the kinds of medical waste that have appeared on beaches or been dumped in trash bins, pozing hazards to human health.

of medical waste. Some states have set up systems to track waste from a medical facility to a disposal site and have established penalties for unsafe handling of medical waste.

States also have enacted legislation that places more rigid controls on industrial producers of hazardous materials. Massachusetts, for example, requires that industries reduce toxic emissions. The state's Department of Environmental Protection provides technical assistance for companies that are slow to cut back toxic waste, and the University of Lowell conducts research on alternatives to toxic chemical use in industry.

On the West Coast, California has set up a hazardous waste management plan that requires each county to make a list of all the businesses and industries that produce hazardous waste and then project how much waste companies will produce through the mid-1990s. Counties also must identify the routes for transporting hazardous waste and analyze the treatment and disposal of toxic materials. The plan calls for counties to encourage recycling and reduction of hazardous waste by developing treatment plants and facilities to reuse such things as solvents and motor oil.

Yet there are major problems and hassles for some small businesses that must meet state guidelines for cleaning up the environment. In one instance, businesswoman Gerry Hassenflug opened a car wash, locating her business in Ventura, California, on property once used as a service station. The business opened in 1982, and six years later Hassenflug learned that a state environmental law required her to have an obsolete underground gasoline tank dug up and removed. The cost was $6,000.

Then soil samples showed the land had been contaminated from leaded gasoline that had spilled during filling operations. The cost to remove the contaminated soil? More than $400,000. Such expenses can destroy a small business and render property almost worthless since few would want to buy or lend money to improve the land. However, California provides financial help for owners of small businesses who are not responsible for past hazardous waste problems but now must clean up their facilities.

If a business person like Hassenflug just walks away and abandons her property, the state would have to take over and pay the cleanup costs. Thus, state lawmakers generally favor tough laws to prevent deliberate environmental pollution.[5]

Cleaning Up

"Are we cleaning up the mess or messing up the cleanup?" is the question the OTA asked in an introduction to case studies of Superfund sites. Although the studies present a bleak picture of most cleanup activities, they also show that some efforts have been fairly successful. Usually, several kinds of treatment are involved in cleanup operations, including waste disposal in mass-burners and detoxifying groundwater (which can take twenty to forty years). Some industries are handling hazardous wastes on site, injecting toxins into deep wells and storing the materials far below the aquifer, or supply of water used for drinking.

In some cases, a technology called in situ vitrification is used—workers insert electrodes into contaminated soil, heating it and turning it into a hard, glassy material. Scientists also are working on ways to clean up toxic wastes with microorganisms. Drs. James Wild and Frank Raushel, who head a research team at Texas A&M University, have discovered a bacterium that produces a special enzyme. The enzyme has an "appetite" for organophosphate compounds (chemicals) commonly used in insecticides to control fire ants, ticks, and other insects. According to the researchers, the enzyme attacks the bonds that hold together molecules of insecticides and nerve toxins. If the molecule's internal bonds are broken, the compound degrades and loses its toxicity. The researchers believe the enzyme will clean up pesticides and obsolete chemical weapons such as nerve gases.

In other experiments, biochemists at Los Alamos National

Laboratory are growing bacteria that "eat" chemical wastes around weapons plants. The researchers hope to find the types of soil best suited to the bacteria and grow them in bulk to transform hazardous chemicals into harmless ones. Similar research is being conducted in university and private laboratories across the nation and in Europe. Scientists have found bacteria that break down poisonous dry-cleaning solvents, PCBs, and other toxins into harmless chemicals.

Exxon Corporation has been involved in a major experiment in Alaska to clean up the oil that spilled from one of its tankers into Prince William Sound. Working with EPA researchers, Exxon has been using bacteria to feed on the oil that contaminates beaches. The process involves applying fertilizers to sections of the shoreline during the warm months. The fertilizers help increase the microbes native to the Alaskan soil. With a much larger number of bacteria, the oil decomposes faster than would occur if the bacteria were allowed to multiply on their own.

What About Household Poisons?

With all the discussion about huge volumes of dangerous waste, it may seem absurd to raise a question about hazardous household products. But many homes can be hazardous waste sites. Household cleaners from drain openers to spot removers, paints, batteries, automotive products (such as antifreeze and brake fluid), and pesticides like insect and mouse killers are among the many products that can endanger human health and the environment.

The majority of consumers toss chemical products into the trash or garbage can along with yard and food wastes. Although hazardous household throwaways make up only a small portion—about one percent—of the waste stream in most communities, the material adds to the already complex problems with waste disposal at landfills.

The words from the opening paragraph of a Greenpeace flyer, "Stepping Lightly on the Earth: Everyone's Guide to Toxics in the Home," put it this way:

Most of us like to think that the widespread contamination of our groundwater, soil and air is entirely due to the irresponsibility of large industry. We refuse to accept the notion that in our own everyday lives we are contributing to the slow poisoning of the planet. But commonly used substances such as paint thinners, household pesticides, cleaners and solvents, and some aerosols produce hazardous waste. Our responsibility for them does not end at our curbside . . . toxic waste comes back to haunt us.

Toxic leachate can contaminate groundwater, or chemical emissions from waste can create air pollutants. It is also common for people to dump old brake fluid, oil, and the like onto the ground, where the chemicals can seep through the soil to contaminate groundwater.

With increasing awareness of pollution problems, communities across the United States have been setting up programs to collect household poisons. These may be once-a-year events or part of

People in communities across the United States organize hazardous waste collection days to collect and properly dispose of hazardous household discards.

ongoing recycling and waste management efforts. Some programs provide information on how to treat hazardous household wastes safely at home or suggest ways that householders can reuse or recycle goods or, better yet, reduce their use of toxic products.

Baking soda, for example, is an all-purpose safe cleaner and deodorizer. Other environmentally safe cleaning and polishing substances include vinegar, salt, washing soda, cream of tartar, lemon (lemon oil for polishing), and ammonia (used with care). Many national magazines and major newspapers have published articles on how to use these substances.

More than 20,000 private companies and institutions use radioactive substances in their daily activities, producing most of the low-level radioactive waste in the United States.

8

Debates Over Nuclear Waste

A series of signs along the road in Nora, a small farm village in Nebraska, read: "Pass this schoolhouse . . . Take it slow . . . Give the children . . . A chance to grow . . . Dump the dump." At the time of this writing, the dump had not yet been located near the village. But it is one of the possible sites for dumping nuclear waste from the southcentral states—Nebraska, Kansas, Oklahoma, Louisiana, and Arkansas. The twenty-seven people who live in Nora do not want the nuclear waste site near their village, and they feel powerless in the face of waste management specialists who have recommended Nora as a disposal site.

Nora is not alone in its opposition to having nuclear waste right next door. Like groups who protest the siting of landfills and incinerators for garbage and trash in their backyards, people in communities across the nation are engaged in heated NIMBY debates over nuclear waste disposal.

The Big Buildup

The problem of nuclear waste disposal has been festering since the United States began to build atomic bombs in the 1940s. At that time, the federal Atomic Energy Commission (AEC) was set up to oversee production of a bomb—an atomic, or nuclear, bomb—that would help end World War II. An atomic bomb explodes because of fission—unstable uranium atoms called isotopes split into parts. As the isotopes split, they release neutrons, tiny atomic particles, which in turn hit other uranium atoms, fissioning them in a continual chain reaction that creates more and more heat and eventually causes an explosion.

After World War II, the United States and Great Britain developed hydrogen bombs, said to be 7,500 times more destructive than atomic bombs. When a hydrogen bomb explodes, atoms split and then join together in a process called fusion that generates vast amounts of energy. The hydrogen bomb has not been used in war, but the United States has continued to build nuclear weapons. It has been a long-standing defense policy of the United States to build enough weapons so that other nations will be afraid to attack, maintaining a so-called balance of terror.

Since World War II, nuclear weapons plants have been built in such states as Washington, Colorado, Ohio, Tennessee, and South Carolina. For more than forty years, atomic reactors at the U.S. Hanford Reservation, Richland, Washington, burned uranium to produce plutonium, which also fissions and is used to make nuclear weapons. (Although plutonium occurs in small amounts in nature, the metal is primarily the by-product of carefully controlled fission in nuclear reactors.) In 1950, reactors at the Savannah River Plant in South Carolina began producing not only plutonium but also another

79

by-product, tritium, a form of hydrogen, used in the manufacture of warheads for nuclear missiles.

Today's nuclear weapons are so numerous and powerful that they could destroy the entire planet. As a result, international efforts have been underway in recent years to reduce the number of nuclear weapons worldwide. At the same time, groups of scientists, engineers, technicians, and others around the globe have continued their work begun in the 1950s to develop peaceful uses of nuclear energy.

Nuclear power plants, for example, produce electricity. The first commercial nuclear power plant in the United States was built in Pennsylvania and began producing electricity in 1957. Since then, commercial nuclear reactors have supplied electrical power for cities across the nation and in other countries, such as Canada, France, Japan, Sweden, and the Soviet Union. Nuclear reactors also produce valuable radioisotopes used in such activities as laboratory research, making clock dials luminous, and detecting tumors or other physical abnormalities in people.

Sources of Nuclear Waste

Whenever radioactive materials are used, they produce waste. Basically, nuclear waste comes from defense-related activities—weapons plants and nuclear-powered ships—and from private industry, including medical facilities, laboratories, and nuclear power plants. Another source of nuclear waste is uranium mining. When uranium ore is processed at a mill, the "tailings," or leftovers, contain small amounts of radioactive elements that occur naturally.

In the United States, the federal government uses six different categories to define nuclear waste. But in broad terms, wastes can be classified as low-level or high-level, depending on how much radioactivity is emitted. Radioactivity begins to take place as soon as an atom splits, releasing energy (radiation) in the form of particles or rays. As the number of atoms decreases, so does the rate of radioactive emission, which is said to decay. The rate of decay is measured by half-life, or the time it takes for half the atoms of a radioactive substance to disintegrate to another nuclear form. Half-lives vary from fractions of a second to billions of years.

What effect does radiation have on people? That depends on the amount of radiation and the length of time a person is exposed. Radiation effects are measured in millirem units. In the United States, the standard "safe" limit for radiation is 500 millirem per person annually. The federal standard is for radiation exposure from sources other than "background radiation" (from the earth's surface and outer space, for example) and from medical procedures such as x-rays.

Most Americans are exposed to an average of 200 millirem radiation per year. This low-level radiation from everyday sources does not appear to cause health problems, although scientists worldwide have debated whether or not low-level radiation over long periods of time creates health risks. As radiation doses increase, the risks to human health appear to increase as well. Large doses of radiation have been linked to cancer and birth defects. Intense radiation kills large numbers of cells and may cause internal bleeding and the failure of vital organs. Exposure to large doses all at once is lethal.

The total volume of nuclear waste in the United States is small compared to that of solid waste—garbage and trash—but some high-level radioactive waste can be extremely dangerous. The nuclear fuel cycle generates most of the highly radioactive material. That cycle begins with mining uranium ore, which is converted to gas and then "enriched," or processed, so that it contains more U-235 atoms—the uranium isotopes that can be split apart easily. Then the gas is turned into a powdered uranium dioxide and formed into small pellets that are placed inside twelve-foot-long, thin tubes called fuel rods. About 200 rods are bundled to form a fuel assembly.

Fuel assemblies make up the core of a nuclear reactor and are surrounded by control rods that absorb neutrons and determine the speed of the fission reaction. When the control rods are in place, fission slows down, but when the rods are pulled out, the speed of the chain reaction increases. Steel and concrete around the core prevent radiation from escaping.

During the fission process, hundreds of different types of by-products are created. These fission products, as they are called, are solids or gases. In addition, when uranium atoms absorb neutrons but do not fission, they become elements known as tranuranics. Plutonium is one of them. Radioactive fission products and transuranics accumulate, but are locked inside the fuel rods.

As fuel assemblies absorb more and more neutrons, fission slows down. Thus every three or four years, the assemblies must be replaced. At federal facilities, spent fuel from nuclear reactors is recycled. That is, the assemblies go to processing plants on the site, and uranium and plutonium are recovered for use in nuclear weapons. Some spent fuel from commercial power plants was meant to be recovered also. But commercial processing plants that operated in the 1960s and 1970s have shut down because of design problems and high costs.

Since some of the by-products in the spent fuel rods remain radioactive for many thousands to millions of years, the assemblies are immediately stored underwater in pools—rather like swimming pools—near the reactors. Water circulates around the assemblies, cooling the spent fuel and acting as a radiation shield. Although some spent fuel rods have been in storage pools since the 1960s, the cooling ponds were meant to serve only as temporary storage facilities until the radioactive material could be treated and placed in a permanent waste disposal site. But developing a place to store high-level nuclear waste has become costly and controversial, and is discussed later in this chapter.

Like landfills, nuclear storage pools are filling up. States where commercial nuclear reactors are located are concerned about what effects these pools may be having on the environment. High-level waste from commercial reactors is regulated by the federal government, but over the years, federal facilities have had a poor track record in regard to management of their own nuclear wastes—materials generated from reactors and weapons plants.[1]

Fallout at Bomb Plants

For more than forty years, nuclear weapons plants were operated in secret with little oversight from Congress or federal regulatory agencies. The facilities were closed to public scrutiny because of what some have called an overzealous concern about national security. When the Atomic Energy Commission was dissolved in 1974, several federal agencies took over responsibilities of nuclear weapons protection and management of nuclear waste. In 1977, the U.S. Department of Energy (DOE) was formed, and one of its main assignments is nuclear research and development, which includes plans for nuclear waste disposal.

In the past, it was common practice to dump some radioactive wastes from the manufacture of weapons directly into burial pits or leaky ponds. According to the conventional wisdom of twenty to thirty years ago, "dilution was the solution to pollution." In other words, the experts theorized that large volumes of air, soil, and water would dilute contaminants so that they would not be hazardous to public health. However, laboratory tests of spring water near the Hanford Reservation in Washington, a weapons plant that was permanently closed in 1988, showed levels of radioactive materials 1,000 times higher than federal standards now allow for drinking water.

DOE oversees and in effect owns nuclear weapons plants but contracts with private companies such as the Westinghouse Corporation, Rockwell International, and the Martin Marietta Corporation to operate the facilities. Since 1987, federal government studies and private investigations have shown that DOE has been lax in its oversight responsibilities. The studies document mechanical failures and lack of safety precautions at weapons plants, plus contamination of the environment from nuclear waste disposal.

One of the worst hazardous waste sites in the United States is within the weapons manufacturing complex known as Rocky Flats near Denver, Colorado. A total of 166 hazardous waste sites are located

83

at Rocky Flats, which makes plutonium triggers for warheads and produces wastes like plutonium dust, a lethal carcinogen.

In 1989, the Department of Justice sent FBI agents to investigate the Rocky Flats plant. Agents found violations of federal environmental laws and charged that plant and DOE officials "knowingly and falsely" stated they were abiding by the laws and were concealing "serious contamination" at the plant site. Contaminants from the site threaten the water supply for Denver area residents, and some workers exposed to plutonium dust believe the radioactive material is linked to cancers they now suffer.

Radioactive and toxic compounds also contaminate the environment near nuclear facilities in Ohio, Tennessee, and South Carolina. At Oak Ridge, Tennessee, for example, a plant known as Y-12 processes uranium for weapons and for more than thirty years dumped liquid wastes into four nearby ponds, which covered five acres. The ponds were contaminated not only with uranium but also with nitrate compounds and mercury that were leaking into soil and groundwater.[2]

High Costs of Cleanup and Storage

Cleanup of the Oak Ridge complex has been going on since 1984, and the DOE has spent $1.2 billion to drain the storage ponds, filling them in with rocks and clay and covering them over with asphalt. A $26 million furnace—the first of its kind—was built to burn some radioactive waste substances such as PCBs and mercury. Other weapons plants in Fernald and Portsmouth, Ohio, and Paducah, Kentucky, will send nuclear wastes to be burned in the furnace also.

According to recent government projections, the Oak Ridge cleanup will not be completed until the mid-1990s at an estimated cost of $19.5 billion. And although radioactive liquid waste at the plant has been reduced almost 75 percent, there are still questions about how to safely dispose of six large tanks of what officials call "extremely hot" radioactive waste that cannot be burned or buried.

Several other weapons facilities have been shut down or partially closed to correct safety violations or to clean up contaminated areas. James Watkins, appointed secretary of the DOE by President George Bush, has said that "the chickens have finally come home to roost," and the department must now clean up federal nuclear facilities in a dozen or more states. Total cleanup costs may reach $130 to $150 billion and will involve varied methods to deal with complex contaminants in soil and water.[3]

Vitrification is one cleanup method. Long used in France, where vitrification first developed, and now in other European countries and Canada, the process involves separating highly radioactive materials (called sludge) from other substances in liquid waste. The radioactive sludge is combined with clay or sand, and the mixture is heated and transformed into molten glass that is poured into steel canisters to harden for storage. In France, high-level wastes produced by nuclear reactors since 1974 have been vitrified to a solid form that now makes up no more volume than an Olympic-size swimming pool.

In the United States, vitrification is part of the cleanup process at West Valley, New York, once the site of a commercial nuclear waste recycling plant that closed in 1972 because of business failure. When the 3,300-acre facility operated, the plant accepted spent fuel assemblies from nuclear reactors, cut up the rods, and put the pieces in acid to dissolve the solid fuel. Then uranium and plutonium were extracted from the liquid, and the remaining solution, which will be radioactive for thousands of years, was stored in an underground tank that has a life span of about forty years. Cleanup, which began in 1982 and may not be completed until the end of the 1990s, includes draining the radioactive waste from the underground tank through filters, then vitrifying the sludgelike material.

A similar process is being used at the closed Hanford Reservation in Washington and at the Savannah River weapons plant in Aiken, South Carolina. A vitrification plant—a gigantic concrete structure—was completed recently at the South Carolina facility, where liquid plutonium wastes have been accumulating since 1950.

Although Savannah River officials believe the radioactive materials will stay locked within the glass (inside steel canisters) forever, members of some environmental groups are not so sure. Yet they believe vitrification is better than leaving the waste in tanks that might explode because of hydrogen buildup. The steel canisters will be stored on site (as will those at West Valley and Hanford) until they can be taken to a permanent storage facility.

Where will that facility be? That is a question many local, state, and federal government officials would like answered—soon. In 1982, Congress passed the Nuclear Waste Policy Act, which mandates a detailed procedure to be completed by 1998 for disposal of high-level nuclear waste in rock formations deep underground. Nuclear scientists and geologists around the world generally agree that isolating the material for thousands of years will protect the environment and people from radiation hazards.

The experts' conclusions are based not only on laboratory analyses and experiments but also on a discovery of a "natural nuclear reactor" that existed 1.8 billion years ago in Africa. Deep underground, a fission chain reaction took place in a vein of uranium ore saturated with water. This natural reactor operated for thousands of years and produced the same kind of radioactive waste produced by nuclear power plants built in this century. Studies of the area have shown that the radioactive materials, including plutonium, remained stable and decayed slowly into nonradioactive elements. Other countries that operate nuclear power systems—Argentina, Canada, France, Italy, Japan, Sweden, and Germany, among them—also plan to dispose of high-level waste in deep underground formations.

In the United States, one planned site was in a Kansas salt bed, but it was abandoned because engineers found oil and gas drillings made it unstable. Another pilot project is located near Carlsbad, New Mexico, far below the desert in rooms carved from salt formations. Called the Waste Isolation Pilot Plant, it is designed to store materials contaminated with plutonium and other long-lived radioactive elements. But the $700 million facility has not opened yet because there is fear that moisture seeping into the caverns will mix with salt and corrode drums holding the nuclear waste.

Still one more storage facility is planned for Yucca Mountain, Nevada, near Las Vegas. The Yucca Mountain site will be the repository for canisters of glassified radioactive materials. However, there are delays here, too, as geologists and engineers debate over whether there will be volcanic activity or water leaks at the site.

What to Do with Low-Level Waste?

All the problems at weapons plants and questions about what to do with highly radioactive nuclear waste have created concerns about the disposal of low-level radioactive waste. Low-level nuclear waste

Investigations of low-level radioactive waste sites entail highly sophisticated samplings of leachate solutions in the buried waste.

includes such things as discarded gloves and clothing used by nuclear plant workers, some resins from power plants, and radioactive materials from hospitals and laboratories. It is the kind of waste that farmers in Nora, Nebraska, want to keep out of their backyard, although experts claim the radioactivity of the waste generally is short-lived.

Because of limited facilities for nuclear waste, federal law now mandates that individual states or a compact (group) of states take responsibility for disposing of low-level nuclear wastes generated within their boundaries. It is an issue that has aroused many NIMBY protests not only in Nora but also in other communities across the nation.

People who live near proposed waste sites fear that their soil and water will be contaminated. However, some environmental and civic groups are taking part in the process of determining where nuclear waste facilities will be located and how they will be designed.

What kinds of facilities are being proposed? Shallow underground burial is one possibility. Basically, airtight containers of low-level nuclear waste would be buried in trenches dug in clay soil and located away from any water flow. The trenches would be lined with sand, gravel, or crushed stone to provide drainage should water or snow melt seep in.

Depending on radiation levels, a remote-controlled crane or a worker-operated fork lift would stack the waste in the trench. Sand would be forced into spaces between the packages and drums to help prevent shifting and allow for a quick flow of any seeping water. Several feet of clay, ten feet of soil, perhaps a cement cap, about a foot of gravel, and another foot-and-a-half of topsoil would form a sloping moundlike cap over the trench. A correctly designed trench cap is the most important safeguard for land burial of low-level nuclear waste, according to the Atomic Industrial Forum, an international association of about 500 organizations working for peaceful uses of nuclear energy. The forum noted that the cap:

shields the environment against direct radiation from buried waste. Most importantly, it prevents large quantities of water from infiltrating down into the trenches, corroding buried packages, dissolving the waste form and transporting radionuclides to the environment.[4]

Another method of handling low-level nuclear waste is to store it in cement shafts sunk into the ground and capped with concrete. Concrete warehouses for storage above ground have been proposed also.

Benefits Versus Risks

Debates over nuclear power and weapons and what to do with radioactive waste will continue through this century and into the next. Some people scoff at the potential dangers of radiation. Dozens of recent newspaper and magazine reports on this issue show that many workers at nuclear facilities are more concerned about maintaining their jobs than about possible health effects from radiation exposure. In areas where jobs are scarce, some people say they would welcome a nuclear waste dump or other nuclear facility that would bring employment opportunities with it.

Part of the nuclear energy controversy revolves around the growing need for electricity and the fact that coal-fired power plants generates pollutants that are partially responsible for such global problems as the greenhouse effect and acid rain. Some air pollutants can be more long-lasting than radioactive materials.

Recently, some opponents of nuclear power have begun to support—very cautiously—the idea that nuclear energy may be necessary. The Union of Concerned Scientists (UCS), for example, has been strongly opposed to present nuclear plants, which the group says are unsafe. But recently the UCS has suggested that "a safer generation of reactors could be designed." However, as Howard Ris, executive director of UCS, explained in a letter to Greenpeace: "We have always included the caveat that before any such new generation might become possible, the nuclear industry must: (a) show that new technologies will eliminate all major risk to public safety; (b) accept stringent and comprehensive regulation; and (c) demonstrate that safe methods exist for the long-term disposal of radioactive waste." Ris added that the UCS has doubts that "the nuclear industry could ever meet such criteria."

Many people fear nuclear energy and the wastes that nuclear plants generate because they believe they will be exposed to high levels of radiation from accidental leaks, citing the 1979 accident at the Three Mile Island reactor in the United States and the 1986 explosion at the Chernobyl plant in the Soviet Union.

At Three Mile Island in Pennsylvania, a faulty valve prevented cooling water from circulating in the reactor, overheating the core and melting more than half of it. As a result, radioactive emissions spewed into the air. But studies later showed that the radiation dose averaged 10 millirems for people within ten miles of the reactor and up to 100 millirems for plant workers. Some experts claim that there is no evidence of increased cancer rates or other health problems due to the radiation, while others argue that cancers generally do not develop for fifteen to twenty years after exposure, and they expect cancer rates in the region to rise.

The world's worst nuclear power plant accident occurred in the Soviet Ukraine, when an explosion and fire destroyed the Chernobyl plant. Highly radioactive clouds spread over Scandinavia, England, and parts of Europe, eventually leaving thirty-one dead and thousands more facing possible health problems because of high doses of radiation.

Proponents of nuclear power, however, agree with the view of the U.S. Department of Energy Secretary James Watkins, who stated recently: "I expect nuclear power to be increasingly viewed as a safe, environmentally benign and economical alternative for meeting our expanding electricity needs."[5]

Those who favor nuclear energy also point out that several hundred nuclear power plants worldwide safely generate electricity.

Many industrialized nations are increasing their use of nuclear power without serious mishaps, proponents emphasize.

Anyone without expertise in this complex issue of nuclear power has a difficult time sorting out the benefits and the hazards. At the same time, the nuclear waste controversy seems to raise more and more questions, with few of them fully answered. But as the League of Women Voters has pointed out in its handbook on nuclear waste, citizens need to make concerted efforts to be informed.

Materials on nuclear energy and waste are available from several federal departments, including the Department of Energy, the Department of Transportation, the Nuclear Regulatory Commission, and the Environmental Protection Agency. Environmental groups also publish materials on the subject. Some selected references are listed at the end of this book. Also listed are various government agencies and environmental groups that can provide information not only on nuclear waste disposal but on other waste problems as well.

Surveys of Americans during the 1990s show that the majority of those polled believe the world faces an environmental crisis.

9

—

The Environmental Decade

"Continue to contaminate your bed and you will one night suffocate in your own waste," an Indian chief warned American settlers in the 1800s. More than 150 years later, the warnings from many sources are ominous, and people in varied walks of life feel that time is running out in terms of saving our planet from all kinds of pollution problems.

"Ours may well be the last generation that has the opportunity to save our natural world and restore those aspects of our global environment we have already degraded," Jay Hair, head of the National Wildlife Federation, told members of NWF at their annual meeting in the spring of 1989. "The 1990s has got to be the decade of the environment," he said.

Hair expressed what many environmentalists, scientists, researchers, and an increasing portion of the general public have asserted. News reporters and commentators also have put the spotlight on environmental problems. "Race to Save the Planet," an excellent series of TV specials (with transcripts available), aired on Public Broadcasting stations and described the causes and effects of such threats as global warming, ozone depletion, acid rain, hazardous chemical wastes, and nuclear wastes. Such topics have been covered as well in issues of national magazines such as *Newsweek*, *Time*, *Scientific American*, *Scholastic*, and *Omni*.

Within the past decade, several magazines dealing with our mounting garbage problems and the need for recycling have been launched. *BioCycle*, a trade journal for waste managers, is published in Emmaus, Pennsylvania, and deals with trash and sludge recycling and municipal composting worldwide. *Resource Recycling* published in Portland, Oregon, is a "nuts-and-bolts" magazine that includes articles about recycling organizations across the United States, what states are doing in regard to recycling laws and programs, and news about recycling equipment and markets for recyclables. A publication from New York is *Garbage: The Practical Journal for the Environment*. It, too, contains many how-to articles, including how to recycle food scraps and yard waste by composting, how to set up a recycling center in the home, and how to choose products with the least amount of packaging. (See **Groups to Contact** for addresses of the magazines.)

Reducing Waste at the Source

Although we are almost inundated with news about widespread environmental problems, there are some encouraging signs. A few major manufacturers are finding ways to generate less waste rather than just trying to deal with by-products that may cause environmental pollution or health hazards. Waste management specialists call it "waste minimization," or "pollution prevention," or "source reduction."

Actions to reduce waste are not always prompted by concerns for the environment, however. "Waste management is the only way to save industry some of the escalating costs of the current waste-management system," wrote Joel Hirschhorn in *Technology Review*. Hirschhorn, who is a senior researcher with Congress's Office of Technology Assessment, has conducted a number of studies on hazardous waste. He reported that the direct costs of disposal have risen several hundred percent since the early 1980s, and will continue to go up as regulations to protect the environment become more strict. Added to that figure are costs for liability suits. Fines for corporations that pollute rose from a total of $300,000 in 1983 to about $12 million in 1989.[1]

Some companies are redesigning products or developing new formulas that do not generate hazardous materials. One simple method of waste reduction involves better "housekeeping" or improvements in plant operations. For example, instead of using hazardous chemicals to clean metal circuits, 3M now uses nontoxic pumice. The company also recycles its metal wastes and sells its plastic wastes to fabricators who make products ranging from plastic auto floor pads to garden hoses.

Reusing waste by-products has been part of AT&T's operations for many years. The company owns a foundry where used copper wire is melted down to make new copper wire, essentially keeping the copper within the company forever. Exxon (the company that was widely criticized because one of its tankers spilled vast amounts of oil off Alaska's shore) sells a waste from plastic manufacturing to a company that makes a material for a caulking product used in mobile homes. Union Carbide (whose subsidiary company in Bhopal, India, leaked hazardous chemicals that killed thousands) claims that its chemical plants across the United States "have reduced the annual amount of hazardous solid wastes requiring treatment or disposal by 64 percent since 1982"—chemical and plastics plants recycle or reuse wastes as substitute raw materials to make other products or to produce energy.

A few major retail businesses in the United States, such as Wal-Mart, are putting green labels on products made by companies that do not pollute the environment. Loblaw, a Canadian food-store chain, is also selling a Green line in its stores, calling the products "environment friendly." Another Canadian franchise company, called The Body Shop, is selling skin- and hair-care products in plastic containers that can be returned for recycling. The British-owned company has more than 350 shops around the world and claims that its products contain no hazardous chemicals.

However, as with all types of advertising claims, buyers must beware. Some companies may simply use terms such as "biodegradable" or "recyclable" to get the environmentally concerned consumer to buy. Watchdog groups—environmental and consumer organizations—uncover and regularly report on misleading advertising in their journals and in news releases to the media. These reports often provide information consumers need to determine what qualifies as "biodegradable" or "recyclable."[2]

"Earth Day Every Day"

As manufacturers, retail businesses, consumers, government regulators, and scientists struggle with ways to reduce waste, there is a growing public recognition that waste disposal represents only one part of interrelated environmental problems. Contaminate the soil and water, and the result may be a poisoned food chain that eventually poses human health hazards. Foul the air near an industry, and pollutants can spread far and wide. People also are recognizing that actions in one part of the world can create global effects. In short, we are gradually learning that we all share in the responsibility of being stewards of the earth.

In April 1970, the first Earth Day was observed to call attention to environmental concerns. During the decade that followed, many laws designed to protect the environment were passed, including the Clean Air Act of 1970, the Water Pollution Control Act of 1972, the Toxic Substances Control Act of 1976, and the Resource Conservation and Recovery Act of 1976. These and other laws helped bring about changes in the manufacturing processes and set the stage for programs to protect the environment. But the administration of President Ronald Reagan (1980–1988) emphasized deregulation, and some officials tried to weaken laws that affected industries.

Yet as the public has learned about the environmental damages linked to heavy consumption and our throwaway lifestyle, they have pressured government officials to pass more stringent regulations to protect our environment. One new measure is the Clean Air Act of 1990 that revises the 1970 law and mandates tighter controls on contaminants emitted into the air from mobile and stationary sources.

Organizations ranging from the Boy Scouts and Girl Scouts to the American Association for Retired People and the League of Women Voters have spread the word about the way people can take action. Religious groups also have taken up the cause, in what has been called a "spiritual ecological movement" that one author predicted would be a major trend in the 1990s.[3]

Indeed, as the new decade began, thousands of groups around the world took part in activities to commemorate Earth Day 1990 and became involved in on-going projects to save our planet's resources. Many groups set up community recycling programs. (Help for such programs in the United States is available from the National Recycling Coalition whose address is listed at the end of this book).

Dozens of books were published during the early 1990s to advise readers on ways they could help save the earth. Environmental organizations such as the National Audubon Society, Friends of the Earth, Environmental Defense Fund, Greenpeace, and Worldwatch Institute, also published a variety of materials on resource conservation, recycling, and waste reduction. The National Wildlife Federation compiled ways that people can observe "Earth Day Every Day"—the organization's theme—through a variety of practical action projects. You can learn more about these projects and those sponsored by any of the other groups by writing to them at addresses listed at the end of the book. Joining a chapter of such a group or supporting an organization with funds is one way to help preserve our planet.

Being an "Activist"

Some young people, have formed their own groups. A prime example is KAP—Kids Against Pollution. The organization got its start in 1987 at Tenakill School in Closter, New Jersey. Nineteen students in Nick Byrne's social studies class had been studying the Bill of Rights, particularly the right of free expression.

"The students decided to use this right by writing letters to editors of newspapers, magazines, and to public officials," Byrne said. "Youngsters wrote on such issues as beach pollution, sewage disposal, recycling, banning of foam products, acid rain, and the greenhouse effect."

Tenakill students also set up a networking organization to gather information about pollution. They elected a board of directors, created a logo for their group, and enlisted the support of other schools in their state and across the nation. To date, several hundred schools representing most of the states and several foreign countries have KAP chapters. KAP kids conduct regular letter-writing campaigns directed at corporate polluters and public officials who can help make changes in the way waste of all kinds is handled. One KAP student who believes that pollution is "the most serious environmental problem today" wrote:

> I think pollution is more deadly than the threat of a nuclear war because everyone knows about the prospect of that war, but pollution just sneaks up behind you. By the time you notice it, it is too late to do anything.[4]

Yet it may not be too late. KAP groups have not only had their say in letter writing but also have prompted cleanup or better waste disposal methods on local and state levels. The Tenakill School Board, for example, listened to KAP kids describe the problems of disposing of nondegradable foam products and decided to buy paper products instead.

In Salt Lake City, Utah, an elementary class that had joined KAP got in touch with the regional EPA office to urge investigation of a waste site near their school where at least 40,000 barrels had been dumped. EPA investigators found that the waste inside the barrels was hazardous—they contained chemicals that had contaminated the soil. After calls and letters to the mayor, the local health department, and the owner of the property, the barrels were removed.

Other KAP projects have included organizing local Clean-Up Days or Hazardous Waste Collections, or encouraging students to save used aluminum foil that can be rolled into a huge ball for recycling, boycotting businesses that pollute, and encouraging local officials to start citywide recycling programs. To get more information about KAP activities, write to the Tenakill School, 275 High Street, Closter, NJ 07624.

In northern Indiana, students have joined the Waste Not Society sponsored by a private waste management company that operates an environmentally safe landfill and processes materials for recycling. The company sets up school and business collection centers for recyclables and conducts educational program on recycling and waste disposal.

Because of the Waste Not Society programs, many students have become "home activists," convincing their families to voluntarily sort waste for recycling or to reduce solid waste and hazardous materials in the home. Students have expressed their environmental concerns to state legislators and managers of fast-food restaurants, urging a ban on foam packaging and the use of more recyclable products.

In response to letters from one class, a state representative wrote:

> Government may step in at some point and say that (foam plastic) should no longer be used, but one of the best methods for making changes is for consumers to take action and contact the corporate headquarters of restaurants . . . With enough consumer pressure, many eating establishments may find an alternative (to foam packaging).

> Currently, Indiana does not have mandatory recycling laws in place, but unless Hoosiers take an active role in voluntary

recycling, legislative mandates could be our only hope. I
encourage you and each member of your family to work at
recycling . . .[5]

Making Yourself Heard in the Marketplace

As the Indiana state representative suggested, consumers can take
individual actions to tackle the huge problem of waste in our society.
Besides lodging protests about packaging, consumers can make
choices in the marketplace to influence producers and packagers.

The Gallup organization recently surveyed more than 1,000
Americans and found that 81 percent of those polled wanted to buy
products packaged in materials that could be recycled. A design and
product development firm, which also conducted a nationwide survey,
came up with similar findings. In addition, the consulting firm reported
that at least half of those surveyed said they would not buy products
that were harmful to the environment. The trend, which began to
sweep Europe, particularly England, several years ago, is expected to
grow steadily in the United States. If you or your family want to make
your statement about reducing waste, try some of these ideas:

Buy products in aluminum cans or glass—the containers can be recycled.
In some communities, certain plastic containers can be recycled, too. If
your community does not have a mandatory recycling program, check
with waste collectors, landfill operators, scrap dealers, or environmental
groups to find out whether voluntary projects are underway. If you do not
take part in a group effort, you may be able to take recyclable materials
to a nearby collection center on your own. Some supermarkets chains
have set up collection centers for recyclables.

Buy products made from recycled paper, such as greeting cards or toilet
paper. A variety of products from breakfast cereal to cleaning pads are
packaged in recycled cardboard containers. When you buy, look for the
recycling symbol—arrows forming a loop—on the packaging. You also
can identify recycled cardboard by its brown or gray color. The National
Aububon Society and Greenpeace are two environmental organizations

that publish greeting cards on 100 percent recycled paper. Manufacturers of recycled paper products publish catalogs of their supplies. An example is Earth Care Paper, P.O. Box 3335, Madison, WI 53704.

Buy products that can be reused, that biodegrade, or that are nontoxic. For example, many families are buying biodegradable disposable diapers or cloth diapers for babies. If you are not sure that the plastic products offered for sale in the store will actually biodegrade, try a mail order firm such as Seventh Generation, 10 Farrell Street, South Burlington, VT 05403, which has tested some plastic products and found that they will break down; their catalog costs $2. Greenpeace also publishes a catalog with some biodegradable products.

Buy in bulk when possible to reduce wasteful packaging. Avoid overpackaged items such a containers with a single serving or nonessential items that may be packed inside five to seven layers of materials (adding greatly to the cost of the products as well). Refuse "extra" packaging for such items as bags of fruit or jugs of milk. Reusable net or canvas bags, which are popular in Europe, can be used instead of paper or plastic bags to carry purchased items. You also can reuse paper bags for shopping or other purposes.

Closing the Loop

Getting into the habit of reusing things is another important way to reduce waste. An example of how one person can reuse items appeared in a *Parade Magazine* story about Justin Lebo's on-going project to help others. Justin, who was thirteen at the time, began rebuilding old bicycles for needy kids. According to the story, Justin has "a mechanical bent" and began tinkering with repairs and rebuilding junk bikes when he was eleven. The first rebuilt bike was for himself, but then he rebuilt two more, using discarded bike frames and new parts that he bought with his own money. Justin gave the bikes to a New Jersey children's home and decided that since he enjoyed making the kids happy with his gifts, he would supply everyone in the home with a bike. He did just that, finding enough junked bikes and funds for parts to rebuild more than twenty bicycles.[6]

Everyone is not mechanically minded like Justin, but that does not prevent a person from reusing products or materials that might otherwise be thrown out. What about old furniture, household appliances, clothing, and tools? Some will be collected by civic groups or organizations such as Goodwill and the Salvation Army, which restore and resell items, earning funds to help needy people. Perhaps there are individuals or small groups in your community who make braided rugs out of old clothing or quilts from scraps of cloth. A woman in Hillsboro, Oregon, collects plastic bread bags and potato sacks to make braided rugs.

For people who live in rural areas or for those who have gardens, composting is an ideal way to reuse kitchen waste. In some European towns, people separate food scraps from other throwaways, placing them in special containers for pickup. The organic wastes go to a composting yard, where the materials break down and later become fertilizer for gardens and farms.

Take yard waste and leaves to a community compost if you do not have one in your own backyard. Or let the grass stay on the lawn—"cut it high and let it lie" as some landscape and gardening experts will tell you.

Many types of containers can be reused. You can store items ranging from audio tapes to rock collections in old shoe boxes, for example. Do you save other types of boxes to reuse for packaging?

Newspapers can be reused for cushioning between items when you are moving or shipping goods. You can also reuse newspapers in a creative way to wrap gifts—the colorful comics section and glossy advertising pages make interesting wrapping paper. You can reduce the amount of paper you use by writing on both sides of a sheet or by using blank sheets of scrap paper for notes. Feed computer paper through a printer a second time for draft copies of letters, school papers, or whatever.

Have you ever decorated empty cans or plastic containers to use as planters or desk organizers? Chipped mugs and glasses can be decorated for the same purposes. You also can use large coffee cans, plastic jugs, or plastic net bags (the kind that potatoes, onions, or citrus fruits come in) to make feeding stations for birds. The National Wildlife Federation publishes a booklet called *Recycle for the Birds* that describes how to make bird feeders out of everything from milk cartons to aluminum pie plates.

If you or your family want to take other actions to recycle and reuse items and reduce waste, you might go full circle and review ideas in the previous chapters. Or use this list as a reminder:

1. Learn where the nearest collection center for recyclables is located and take your aluminum cans, glass, paper, and perhaps some plastics there. Take seriously the Environmental Defense Fund slogan: "If you're not recycling, you're throwing it all away."

2. Reduce the use of poisonous household cleaners and other products that produce hazardous waste; try to substitute nontoxic substances whenever you can.

3. Avoid using materials made of plastics that do not biodegrade.

4. Repair things you own that could still be useful.

5. Write letters to legislators at the local, state, and federal levels and urge action on laws that will protect the environment.

6. Write opinion pieces or letters to the editor of your local newspaper, expressing your concern about any local or state waste disposal or other environmental problem.

7. Support an environmental organization or start a local group to work on environmental problems.

8. Talk to neighbors, friends, and relatives about our throwaway society and what can be done to reduce waste.

9. Be a smart shopper. Learn which companies produce goods and services that do not harm the environment and buy from them.

10. Educate yourself as much as you can on environmental issues, reading or listening to all sides of an issue (seldom is there one simple way to resolve any waste or pollution problem).

11. Remember that we do not occupy this earth alone. We share it with many other humans and living creatures. If we foul our own nest, do we have a right to let our waste spill over into someone else's backyard or another creature's habitat?

Finally, it comes down to the basic recognition that the more we consume, the more natural resources we use up, the more waste we generate and the more pollution problems we create for our particular space on earth and for the planet as a whole. So each of us can make a difference by reducing, reusing, and recycling waste. No one wants to be buried or destroyed by the stuff. The KAP kids said it well in their motto: "Save the Earth, not just for us but for future generations."

CHAPTER NOTES

Chapter 1

1. As reported by Barbara Wickens with Deborra Schug, "The Throw-Away Society," *Maclean's* (September 5, 1988), pp. 46–47.

2. The National Solid Wastes Management Association, "At A Glance" fact sheet (1989).

3. Joseph F. Sullivan, "New Jersey Thinks Again About Its Hard Line on Trash," *The New York Times* (August 20, 1989), p. E24.

4. John Seymour and Herbert Girardet, *Blueprint for a Green Planet: Your Practical Guide for Restoring the Earth* (New York: Prentice-Hall, 1987), pp. 174–175.

Chapter 2

1. Based on EPA statistics.

2. Vicky Cahan, "Waste Not, Want Not? Not Necessarily," *Business Week* (July 17, 1989), pp. 116–117.

3. Bill Paul, "For Recyclers, the News Is Looking Bad," *The Wall Street Journal* (August 31, 1989), p. B2.

4. Ken Stump and Kathy Dorion, "The System Works: Seattle's Recycling Success," *Greenpeace* (February, 1989), pp. 16–17.

Chapter 3

1. Peter Von Stackelberg, "White Wash: The Dioxin Cover-Up," *Greenpeace* (March/April, 1989), pp. 7–11.

2. Alcoa Recycling Company, "Aluminum Can Recycling Across America" brochure (1990).

3. Steel Can Recycling Institute, "Steel: It's a Natural Friend of the Environment" (undated fact sheet).

Chapter 4

1. Jackie Campbell, "Ed Asner Remembers His Own Junkyard Days," *South Bend Tribune* (November 20, 1988), p. C6.

2. Steel Can Recycling Institute, "Steel: It's a Natural Friend of the Environment" (undated fact sheet).

3. Institute of Scrap Recycling Industries, "ISRI Fact Sheet" (undated).

4. Institute of Scrap Recycling Industries, "Design for Recycling," *Phoenix Quarterly* (Winter 1989), entire issue.

Chapter 5

1. Thomas W. Lippman, "Garbage: Fuel of the Future?" *The Washington Post* (November 13, 1989), p. F1.

2. Telephone interview and news releases.

3. American Petroleum Institute, "Recycling Used Motor Oil" booklet (December 1988), pp. 1–2.

4. Ibid.

5. From a conference presentation by John W. Schwartz, Jr. in March 1989.

Chapter 6

1. Robert Pool, "In Search of the Plastic Potato," *Science* (September 15, 1989), pp. 1187–1189.

2. Tom Watson, "Polystyrene Recycling: Big Money, Big Implications," *Resource Recycling* (September 1989) pp. 24–25, 56–58.

3. Scott Hume, "The Green Revolution—McDonald's," *Advertising Age* (January 29, 1991), p. 32.

4. Ted Allen, "Big Pack Attack," *Science World* (March 8, 1991), p. 2.

Chapter 7

1. *The U.S. Military's Toxic Legacy: America's Worst Environmental Enemy* (Executive Summary), Boston, Mass.: National Toxic Campaign Fund, 1991.

2. D'Vera Cohn "Avtex's Legacy: Big Cleanup Bills, Questions," *The Washington Post* (November 19, 1989), p. A1.

3. Rae Tyson and Julie Morris, "The Chemicals Next Door," *USA Today* (July 31, 1989) pp. A1–A2. Also see: D'Vera Cohn, "Environmental Group Ranks Toxic Polluters," *The Washington Post* (August 11, 1989), p. A10.

4. Dialog (computer information service), United Press International news story, released August 28, 1989.

5. Resources for this section are UPI news stories, July 14, 1989; August 28, 1989; October 6, 1989; October 20, 1989 and several news stories in *The Star-Free Press*, Ventura California, January and February, 1988.

Chapter 8

1. The League of Women Voters Education Fund, *The Nuclear Waste Primer: Handbook for Citizens* (New York: Nick Lyons Books, 1985), p. 30.

2. Mark Miller, "Trouble at Rocky Flats," *Newsweek* (August 14, 1989), pp. 19–20. Also see: Douglas Jehl, "Two Towns Share Flawed Nuclear Plants, Little Else," *Los Angeles Times* (February 12, 1989), pp. 1, 25–27.

3. Thomas Lippman, "Cleaning up 'The Witches' Caldron'," *The Washington Post* (September 6, 1989), p. A4.

4. George D. Russ, Jr., *Low Level Radioactive Waste: Building a Perspective* (Bethesda, Md.: Atomic Industrial Forum, 1986), p. 24.

5. As quoted in "Quotelines," *USA Today* (December 4, 1989), p. 12A.

Chapter 9

1. Joel S. Hirschhorn, "Cutting Production of Hazardous Waste," *Technology Review* (April 1988), pp. 53–61. Also see: Ginny Carroll, "Getting with the Cleanup," *Newsweek* (September 25, 1989), p. 35.

2. Brian Bremner, "A New Sales Pitch: The Environment," *Business Week* (July 24, 1989), p. 50. Also see: "The Green Revolution," *Advertising Age* (January 29, 1991), entire issue.

3. Pat Stone, series of articles in *Mother Earth News* (January/February, May/June, July/August, 1989).

4. As quoted in materials supplied by KAP, Tenakill School, 275 High Street, Closter, N.J. 07624.

5. Letter from Philip T. Warner, Indiana State Representative, November 28, 1989.

6. William Barnhill, "The Best Gift A Kid Could Get," *Parade Magazine* (December 24, 1989), pp. 10–11.

Further Reading

Books and Booklets

Alcoa's Guide to Starting a Successful Aluminum Can Recycling Activity. Pittsburgh, Penn.: Alcoa Recycling Company, November 1988.

Bear, Becky. *Recycle Alaska.* Juneau, Alaska: Alaska Department of Environmental Conservation, 1982.

Bennett, Robert A. *Market Research on Plastics Recycling* (Technical Report #31). Piscataway, N.J.: Rutgers University, 1989.

Connecticut Citizens Action Group & the Connecticut Department of Environmental Protection. *Recycling Primer: Getting Back to Basics.* Hartford, Conn.: Department of Environmental Protection, 1988.

Council on Economic Priorities. *Shopping for a Better World.* New York: Council on Economic Priorities, 1989.

Crampton, Norm. *Complete Trash: The Best Way to Get Rid of Practically Everything Around the House.* New York: M. Evans and Company, 1989.

Earthworks Group. *50 Simple Things You Can Do to Save the Earth.* Berkeley, Calif.: Earthworks Press, 1989.

Facts About Low-Level Radiation. Vienna, Austria: International Atomic Energy Agency, 1981.

Gay, Kathlyn. *Air Pollution.* New York: Franklin Watts, 1991.

———. *Bug Off! Cleaning Nature Naturally.* New York: Walker and Company, 1991.

———. *Water Pollution*. New York: Franklin Watts, 1990.

Goldsmith, Edward and Nicholas Hildyard, eds. *The Earth Report*. Los Angeles: Price Stern Sloan, 1988.

Hallowell, Anne, et al. *Recycling Study Guide*. Madison, Wis.: Bureau of Information and Education, Wisconsin Department of Natural Resources, 1988.

Hawkes, Nigle. *Nuclear Power*. New York and Toronto: Gloucester Press, 1984.

Here Today, Here Tomorrow: A Teacher's Guide to Solid Waste Management. Trenton, N.J.: New Jersey Department of Environmental Protection (undated).

How To Recycle Waste Paper. New York: American Paper Institute, 1989.

Keep America Beautiful (Annual Review). Stamford, Conn.: Keep America Beautiful, 1988.

Landfill Capacity in the Year 2000. Washington, D.C.: National Solid Wastes Management Association, 1989.

League of Women Voters Education Fund. *The Nuclear Waste Primer: A Handbook for Citizens*. New York: Nick Lyons Books, 1985.

Lefkowitz, R.J. *Save It! Keep It! Use It Again!* New York: Parents' Magazine Press, 1977.

Lewis, Sanford and Marco Kaltofen. *From Poison to Prevention: A White Paper on Replacing Hazardous Waste Facility Siting With Toxics Reduction*. Boston, Mass.: The National Toxics Campaign Fund, 1989.

Military Toxics Network. *The U.S. Military's Toxic Legacy: America's Worst Environmental Enemy* (Executive Summary). Boston, Mass.: National Toxic Campaign Fund, 1991.

Newsday staff. *Rush to Burn: Solving America's Garbage Crisis?* Covelo, Cal.: Island Press, 1988.

Nuclear Power and the Environment Book 4; Questions and Answers. LaGrange Park, Ill.: American Nuclear Society, 1982.

O'Connor, Karen. *Garbage.* St. Paul, Minn.: Lucent Books/Greenhaven Press, 1989.

O'Hara, Kathryn J., Suzanne Iudicello, and Rose Bierce. *A Citizens Guide to Plastics in the Ocean: More Than a Litter Problem.* Washington, D.C.: Center for Environmental Education, 1988.

Plastics in the Waste Stream: Options for Practical Solid Waste Management. Wayne, N.J.: The Vinyl Institute, 1988.

Plastics Recycling Directory. Washington, D.C.: Plastic Bottle Institute, 1989.

Pringle, Laurence. *Nuclear Energy: Troubled Past, Uncertain Future.* New York: Macmillan, 1989.

———. *Restoring Our Earth.* Hillside, N.J.: Enslow Publishers, 1987.

———. *Throwing Things Away: From Middens to Resource Recovery.* New York: Thomas Y. Crowell, 1986.

Questions Kids Ask About Energy. Madison, Penn.: Westinghouse Electric Corporation, 1981.

Recycling Used Motor Oil: A Model Program. Washington, D.C.: American Petroleum Institute, 1988.

Recycling: Do It Today for Tomorrow. Chicago: Amoco Chemical Company, 1989.

Russ, George D., Jr., *Low-Level Radioactive Waste: Building a Perspective.* Bethesda, Md.: Atomic Industrial Forum, 1986.

Scrap: America's Ready Resource. Washington, D.C.: Institute of Scrap Recycling Industries (undated).

Seymour, John, and Herbert Girardet. *Blueprint for a Green Planet:*

Your Practical Guide to Restoring the World's Environment. New York: Prentice Hall, 1987.

Steel Recycling—A New Era. Pittsburgh, Penn.: Steel Can Recycling Institute (undated).

The Great Glass Caper. Washington, D.C.: Glass Packaging Institute, 1987.

The Management of Radioactive Wastes. Vienna, Austria: International Atomic Energy Agency, 1981.

Toward Environmental Excellence: A Progress Report. Danbury, Conn.: Union Carbide Corporation, December 1989.

Treasure in Our Trash. Washington, D.C.: National Solid Wastes Management Association, 1988.

U.S. Office of Technology Assessment. *Are We Cleaning Up? 10 Superfund Case Studies.* Washington, D.C.: U.S. Government Printing Office, June 1988.

Wild, Russell, ed. *The Earth Care Annual 1991.* Emmaus, Penn.: Rodale Press, 1991.

Willcox, Charlotte. *Trash!* Minneapolis: Carolrhoda, 1989.

Articles

Abrams, Isabel S. "At Your Disposal: Waste Management in the '80s" *Current Health 2*, March 1988, pp. 9–11.

Allen, Ted. "Big Pack Attack." *Science World*, March 8, 1991, p. 2.

Alvarez, Robert, and Arjun Makhijani. "Nuclear Waste: The $100 Billion Mess." *The Washington Post*, September 4, 1988, p. C3.

Barnhill, William. "The Best Gift a Kid Could Get." *Parade Magazine*, December 24, 1989, pp. 10–11.

"Battle of the Bottle." *Time*, June 5, 1989, p. 49.

Beck, Melinda, et al. "Buried Alive." *Newsweek*, November 27, 1989, pp. 66–76.

Begley, Sharon, with Theresa Waldrop. "Microbes to the Rescue!" *Newsweek*, June 19, 1989, pp. 56–57.

Booth, William, and D'Vera Cohn. "Sharing the Environmental Burden." *The Washington Post*, April 18, 1990, p. A1.

Bremner, Brian. "A New Sales Pitch: The Environment." *Business Week*, July 24, 1989, p. 50.

Bremner, Brian, with Pia Farrell. "Europe's Garbage Smells Sweet to Waste Management." *Business Week*, May 29, 1989, p. 33.

Brown, Paul B. "Plastics!" *INC.*, June 1990, pp. 70–77.

Budiansky, Stephen. "Uncle Sam's Risky Bomb Plants." *U.S. News & World Report*, May 25, 1987, pp. 75–76.

Budiansky, Stephen, with William J. Cook. "The Year the Bomb Makers Went Boom." *U.S. News & World Report*, October 31, 1988, pp. 35–36.

Cahan, Vicky. "Waste Not, Want Not? Not Necessarily." *Business Week*, July 17, 1989, pp. 116–117.

Carroll, Ginny. "Getting With the Cleanup." *Newsweek*, September 25, 1989, p. 35.

Charles, Dan. "Will These Lands Ne'er Be Clean?" *New Scientist*, June 24, 1989, pp. 36–37.

Chisholm, Patricia, with John Daly. "Greening the Profits." *Maclean's*, November 7, 1988, pp. 40–41.

Church, George J., Steven Holmes, and Elizabeth Taylor. "Garbage, Garbage, Everywhere." *Time*, September 5, 1988, pp. 81–82.

Clark, Matt, et al. "The Garbage Health Scare." *Newsweek*, July 20, 1987, p. 56.

Coco, Matthew. "Plastics: Concerns about a Modern Miracle." *EPA Journal*, January/February 1988, pp. 41–42.

Cohn, D'Vera. "Avtex's Legacy: Big Cleanup Bills, Questions." *The Washington Post*, November 19, 1989, p. A1.

————. "Environmental Group Ranks Toxic Polluters." *The Washington Post*, August 11, 1989, p. A10.

Commoner, Barry. "Why We Have Failed." *Greenpeace*, September/October, 1989, pp. 12–13.

Conner, Daniel Keith, and Robert O'Dell. "The Tightening Net of Marine Plastics Pollution." *Environment*, January/February 1988, pp. 16–36.

Cook, James. "Breaking the Garbage Blockade." *Forbes*, November 14, 1988, pp. 98–104.

————. "The Garbage Game." *Forbes*, October 21, 1989, pp. 121–130.

Crawford, Mark. "DOE Calls in the Labs for Defense Waste Cleanup." *Science*, October 6, 1989, pp. 24–25.

DEBATE page (on nuclear waste). *USA Today*, December 4, 1989, p. 12A.

Donnelly, John. "Degradable Plastics: Are They a Delusion, a Solution, or a Downright Hoax?" *Garbage*, May/June 1990, pp. 42–47.

Easterbrook, Gregg. "Cleaning Up." *Newsweek*, July 24, 1989, pp. 26–42.

Feder, Barnaby J. "'Mr. Clean' Takes on the Garbage Mess." *The New York Times*, March 11, 1990, pp. B1, B3.

Fisher, Arthur. "Next Generation Nuclear Reactors: Dare We Build Them?" *Popular Science*, April 1990, pp. 68–77.

Forester, William S. "Solid Waste: There's a Lot More Coming." *EPA Journal*, May 1988, pp. 11–12.

Forsch, Robert A., and Nicholas E. Gallopoulos. "Strategies for Manufacturing." *Scientific American*, September 1989, pp. 144–152.

Golay, Michael W. "Longer Life for Nuclear Plants." *Technology Review*, May/June 1990, pp. 25–30.

Grossman, Dan, and Seth Shulman. "Down in the Dumps." *Discover*, April 1990, pp. 36–41.

Hammer, Joshua, with Elizabeth Bradburn. "The Big Haul in Toxic Waste." *Newsweek*, October 3, 1988, pp. 38–39.

Hanley, Robert. "A Second Life for Plastic Cups? Science Turns Them into Lumber." *The New York Times*, February 22, 1989, pp. B1, B4.

Hedstrom, Elizabeth. "Earth Day." *National Parks*, March/April 1990, pp. 18–23.

Hirschhorn, Joel S. "Cutting Production of Hazardous Waste." *Technology Review*, April 1988, pp. 53–61.

Hogan, Barbara. "All Baled Up and No Place to Go." *The Conservationist.* January/February 1988, pp. 37–39.

Holusha, John. "Making the Town Dump Sanitary." *The New York Times*, September 13, 1989, p. C4.

————. "Scientists Are Proving That Natural Plastic is Not an Oxymoron." *The New York Times*, October 21, 1990, p. F9.

Jehl, Douglas. "Two Towns Share Flawed Nuclear Plants, Little Else." *Los Angeles Times*, February 12, 1989, pp. 1, 25–27.

Jones, Peter M. "Is Time Running Out?" *Scholastic Update*, April 21, 1989, p. 2.

Kluger, Jeffrey. "The Residue of Nuclear Hubris." *Discover*, January 1989, pp. 10–11.

Kunes, Ellen. "The Trashing of America." *Omni*, February 1988, pp. 40–44; 92–96.

Langer, Gary. "And Many Happy Returns." *Sierra*, March/April 1988, p. 19–25.

Langone, John. "A Stinking Mess." *Time,* January 2, 1989, pp. 44–47.

Lawren, Bill. "Getting into a Heap of Trouble." *National Wildlife,* August/September 1988, pp. 19–24.

Leinster, Colin. "The Sweet Smell of Profits from Trash." *Fortune,* April 1, 1985, pp. 150–154.

Lief, Louise, John Barnes, and Tana Zulueta. "Dirty Job, Sweet Profits." *U.S. News & World Report,* November 21, 1988, pp. 54–56.

Lippman, Thomas. "Canisters of Glass Hold U.S. Hopes for Plutonium Waste Disposal." *The Washington Post,* November 7, 1989, p. A3.

———. "Cleaning Up 'The Witches' Caldron'." *The Washington Post,* September 6, 1989, p. A4.

———. "Garbage: Fuel of the Future?" *The Washington Post,* November 13, 1989, p. F1.

———. "New Nuclear Waste Facility Proposed." *The Washington Post,* October 21, 1988, p. A13.

———. "Plans for 'Low-Level' Nuclear Dumps Generate Growing Citizen Opposition." *The Washington Post,* July 31, 1989, p. A6.

Luoma, Jon R. "Trash Can Realities." *Audubon,* March 1990, pp. 86-103.

McAllister, Bill. "EPA to Become More Aggresive." *The Washington Post,* June 15, 1989, p. A10.

MacFadyen, J. Tevere. "Where Will All The Garbage Go?" *The New Yorker,* March 1985, pp. 29–38.

Maddocks, Melvin. "No Deposit, No Return." *World Monitor,* May 1988, pp. 14–15.

Main, Jeremy. "Here Comes the Big New Cleanup." *Fortune,* November 21, 1988, pp. 102–118.

Maney, Kevin. "Companies Make Products Nicer to Nature." *USA Today*, August 23, 1989, pp. B1-2.

Mann, Carolyn. "Garbage In, Garbage Out." *Sierra*, September/ October 1987, pp. 22–27.

Manning, Anita. "Communities Pitch in to Cut Garbage." *USA Today*, November 1, 1989, p. 1D.

Marbach, William D., Susan E. Katz, and Dody Tsiantar. "What to Do With Our Waste." *Newsweek*, July 27, 1987, pp. 51–52.

Marinelli, Janet. "Garbage at the Grocery." *Garbage*, September/October, 1989, pp. 34–39.

———. "Packaging." *Garbage*, May/June 1990, pp. 28–33.

Miller, Mark. "Trouble at Rocky Flats." *Newsweek*, August 14, 1989, pp. 19–20.

Monastersky, R. "More Questions Plague Nuclear Waste Dump." *Science News*, June 24, 1989, p. 389.

Nichols, Bill. "Nuclear Waste 'Crisis' Continues, Group Says." *USA Today*, September 19, 1989, p. 10A.

O'Leary, Philip R., Patrick W. Walsh, and Robert K. Ham. "Managing Solid Waste." *Scientific American*, December 1988, pp. 36–42.

Paul, Bill. "For Recyclers, the News Is Looking Bad." *The Wall Street Journal*, August 31, 1989, p. B2.

Pool, Robert. "In Search of the Plastic Potato." *Science*, September 15, 1989, pp. 1187–1189.

Poore, Jonathan. "Kitchen Design for Recycling." *Garbage*, September/October 1989, pp. 18–24.

Porter, J. Winston. "Our Garbage Problem Won't Go Away By Itself." *Chemecology*, September 1989, pp. 3–5.

Ralof, Janet. "The Growing Garbage Mess." *World Book Science Year Book 1990*, pp. 57–67.

Remba, Zev. "Recycle First: Countering the Rush to Burn." *Clean Water Action News*, Winter 1989, pp. 6–7.

Richards, Keith. "All Gas and Garbage." *New Scientist*, June 3, 1989, pp. 38–41.

Roberts, Leslie. "Discovering Microbes with a Taste for PCBs." *Science*, August 28, 1987, pp. 975–977.

Robotham, Rosemarie. "Not in My Backyard." *Omni*, September 1989, pp. 60–64, 92.

Salholz, Eloise, with Peter McKillop. "The Next Love Canal?" *Newsweek*, August 7, 1989, p. 28.

Schwartz, John, et al. "Turning Trash into Hard Cash." *Newsweek*, March 14, 1988, pp. 36–37.

Sheets, Kenneth R., and Robert F. Black. "Generating Cash From Trash." *U.S. News & World Report*, August 22, 1988, pp. 38–40.

Simon, Ruth. "Alchemy, 1990s Style." *Forbes*, July 24, 1989, pp. 92–94.

Smith, Randolph B. "Ecology Claims for Plastic Bags Are Discarded." *The Wall Street Journal*, March 30, 1990, pp. B1, B3.

Sombke, Laurence. "Cut the Garbage." *USA Weekend*, April 21–23, 1989, pp. 4–5.

Spencer, Cathy. "Help Wanted: An Activist's Guide to a Better Earth." (supplement to *Omni* magazine) September 1989.

Steinhart, Peter. "Down in the Dumps." *Audubon*, May 1986, pp. 104–109.

Stevens, William K. "Degradable Plastics Show Promise." *The New York Times*, April 11, 1989, pp. C1 & C12.

———. "When the Trash Leaves the Curb: New Methods Improve Recycling." *The New York Times*, May 2, 1989, pp. C1, C6.

Stone, Pat. Series of articles on spiritual environmentalism. *Mother*

Earth News, January/February 1989, pp. 58–61; May/June 1989, pp. 56-61; July/August 1989, pp. 58–63.

Stump, Ken, and Kathy Dorion. "The System Works: Seattle's Recycling Success." *Greenpeace*, February 1989, pp. 16–17.

Sullivan, Joseph F. "New Jersey Thinks Again About Its Hard Line on Trash," *The New York Times*, August 20, 1989, p. E24.

Taylor, Ronald A., Cynthia Kyle, Dan Collins, and Deborah Kalb. "Another Day Older and Deeper in Trash." *U.S. News & World Report*, May 11, 1987, pp. 20–21.

Thayer, Ann M. "Solid Waste Concerns Spur Plastic Recycling Efforts." *Chemical & Engineering News*, January 30, 1989, pp. 7–15.

"The Chemicals Next Door," a series of articles. *USA Today*, July 31, 1989, pp. 1A–3A; August 1, 1989, p. 6A–7A.

"The Green Revolution," *Advertising Age*, January 29, 1991, entire issue.

Thompson, Terri, and Mimi Bluestone. "Garbage: It Isn't the Other Guy's Problem Anymore." *Business Week*, May 25, 1987, pp. 150–154.

Trippett, Frank, with Don Winbush. "Give Me Your Wretched Refuse." *Time*, November 23, 1987, p. 95.

Turque, Bill, Mary Hager, and David C. Kotok. "Nebraska's New Favorite Son." *Newsweek*, July 10, 1989, p. 21.

"Use It Up—Wear It Out—Make It Do." *The Conservationist*, January/February, 1989, pp. 40–43.

Von Moltke, Konrad. "Challenging the International Order: The 'Greening' of European Politics." *Harvard International Review*. Summer 1990, pp. 22–24.

Von Stackelberg, Peter. "White Wash: The Dioxin Cover-Up." *Greenpeace*, March/April 1989, pp. 7–11.

Wald, Matthew. "A Hitch in Plans for Nuclear Posterity." *The New York Times*, February 12, 1989, p. E7.

———. "Costs Grow and Promise Fades in Nuclear Cleanup." *The New York Times*, October 29, 1989, pp. A1, A34.

———. "Running Out of Space for Nuclear Waste." *The New York Times*, October 22, 1989, p. E7.

Waters, Tom. "The Plastics Problem." *Discover*, February 1989, pp. 22–23.

Watson, Tom. "Polystyrene Recycling: Big Money, Big Implications." *Resource Recycling*, September 1989, pp. 24–25, 56–58.

Weisskopf, Michael. "Plastic Reaps a Grim Harvest in the Oceans of the World." *Smithsonian*, March 1988, pp. 59–66.

Wickens, Barbara, with Deborra Schug. "The Throw-Away Society." *Maclean's*, September 5, 1988, pp. 46–47.

Williamson, Lonnie. "Throwing It All Away." *Outdoor Life*, August 1988, pp. 32–34.

Witkin, Gordon. "The New Midnight Dumpers." *U.S. News & World Report*, January 9, 1989, p. 57.

Wittig, Pat. "Persistent Peril." *Organic Gardening*, February 1989, pp. 66–72.

Groups to Contact

Alcoa Recycling Company
1501 Alcoa Building
Pittsburgh, PA 15219.

The Aluminum Association
818 Connecticut Avenue, NW
Washington, DC 20006.

American Nuclear Energy Council
410 First Street, SE
Washington, DC 20003.

American Paper Institute, Inc.
260 Madison Avenue,
New York, NY 10016.

American Petroleum Institute
1220 L Street, NW
Washington, DC 20005.

Amoco Chemical Company
200 East Randolph Drive
MC4106, Department M082
Chicago, IL 60601.

Atomic Industrial Forum, Inc.
7101 Wisconsin Avenue
Bethesda, MD 20814.

Can Manufacturers Institute
1625 Massachusetts Ave., NW
Washington, DC 20036.

Center for Plastics Recycling Research
Rutgers, The State University of New Jersey
Busch Campus, Bldg. 3529,
Piscataway, NJ 08855.

Center for Science in the Public Interest
1755 S. Street, NW
Washington, DC 20009.

Citizen's Clearinghouse for Hazardous Wastes
P.O. Box 926
Arlington, VA 22216.

Council on Economic Priorities
30 Irving Place
New York, NY 10003.

Dow Chemical Company
Plastics Public Affairs Dept.
2040 Willard H. Dow Center
Midland, MI 48674.

Environmental Defense Fund
257 Park Avenue South
New York, NY 10016.

Friends of the Earth
530 Seventh Street, SE
Washington, DC 20003.

Glass Packaging Institute
1801 K Street, NW
Suite 1105L
Washington, DC 20006.

Greenpeace USA
1436 U Street, NW
Washington, DC 20009.

Institute of Scrap Recycling Industries, Inc.
1627 K Street, NW
Washington, DC 20006.

International Atomic Energy Agency
Wagramerstrasse 5, A-1400
P.O. Box 100
Vienna, Austria.

Keep America Beautiful, Inc.
9 West Broad Street
Stamford, CT 06902.

National Audubon Society
950 Third Avenue
New York, NY 10022.

National Recycling Coalition
1101 30th Street, NW
Washington, DC 20007.

National Solid Wastes Management Association
1730 Rhode Island Ave., NW
Suite 1000
Washington, DC 20036.

The National Toxics Campaign Fund
37 Temple Place, 4th Floor
Boston, MA 02111.

National Wildlife Federation
1400 Sixteenth Street, NW
Washington, DC 20036-2266.

Natural Resources Defense Council
40 East Twentieth Street
New York, NY 10011.

The Nature Conservancy
1800 N. Kent Street, Suite 800
Arlington, VA 22209.

Sierra Club
730 Polk Street
San Francisco, CA 94109.

The Society of the Plastics Industry
1275 K Street, NW
Suite 400
Washington, DC 20005.

Steel Can Recycling Institute
Foster Plaza 10
680 Andersen Drive
Pittsburgh, PA 15220.

Student Environmental Action Coalition
University of North Carolina
CB #5115, Room 102
YMCA Building,
Chapel Hill, NC 21599.

Union of Concerned Scientists
1346 Connecticut Avenue, NW
Washington, DC 20036.

U.S. Committee for Energy Awareness
1735 I Street, NW
Suite 500
Washington, DC 20006.

U.S. Department of Energy
Division of Waste Treatment
Projects
19901 Germantown Road
Germantown, MD 20874.

U.S. Environmental Protection Agency
Office of Solid Waste
401 M Street, SW
Washington, DC 20460.

U.S. Nuclear Regulatory Commission
Office of Nuclear Material Safety and Safeguards
1717 H Street, NW
Washington, DC 20555.

The Vinyl Institute
Wayne Interchange Plaza II
155 Route 46 West
Wayne, NJ 07470.

Worldwatch Institute
1776 Massachusetts Avenue
Washington, DC 20036.

Magazines

BioCycle: Journal of Waste Recycling
Box 351, 18 South Seventh St.
Emmaus, PA 18049.

Garbage: The Practical Journal for the Environment
Old House Journal Corporation
435 Ninth Street
Brooklyn, NY 11215.

E Magazine
P.O. Box 6667
Syracuse, NY 13217.

Mother Earth News
P.O. Box 3122
Harlan, IA 51593-2188.

New Age Journal
P.O. Box 53275
Boulder, CO 80321-3275.

Resource Recycling: North America's Recycling Journal
P.O. Box 10540
Portland, OR 97210.

Glossary

acid rain—Wet or dry deposits of acidic substances.

biodegradable—The property of a substance that allows microorganisms to break it down into simple, stable compounds.

bottle bill—A proposed law to encourage recycling by requiring deposits on beverage containers such as glass bottles, cans, and plastic bottles.

carcinogen—A cancer-causing substance.

CFCs—Chlorofluorocarbons, or chlorine-based gas compounds used in refrigeration, as propellants, and in the manufacture of foam materials.

composting—Creating an environment for food scraps, yard wastes, and similar materials to decay into fertile humus.

conservation—The wise use of natural resources to reduce waste and loss.

cullet—Crushed glass.

dioxins—A group of 75 related chemical compounds that form during manufacturing processes or incineration of various waste products. Some dioxins are extremely toxic and carcinogenic.

dump—An uncontrolled site for disposing of waste now banned in most areas.

enzyme—A protein that brings about chemical reactions or changes.

ferrous scrap—Scrap metal materials that contain iron or steel.

fission—The process of splitting into parts; in a nuclear reaction, an atom fissions or splits into fragments.

half-life—The time it takes for a radioactive substance to lose 50 percent of its activity.

hazardous waste—Waste that is toxic or explosive, can burn easily, or dissolves metal or flesh; such waste causes environmental and human health problems.

HDPE—High-density polyethylene, a type of plastic resin used primarily to make milk jugs and bases of large soft-drink containers.

humus—Soil from decayed vegetable matter that provides valuable nutrients for plants.

incinerator—A waste burner.

leachate—Any liquid and components within it that drain from a landfill or other site where people have placed materials.

leaching—The removal of various substances as water moves through soil.

LDPE—Low-density polyethylene, a type of plastic resin used to make film food wrap.

microbe—A minute organism.

nonferrous scrap—Scrap metal that does not contain iron or steel, such as aluminum, copper, lead, or nickel.

nuclear waste—Waste from nuclear weapons and power plants and a variety of products that contain radioactive materials.

organic—Waste from living organisms; usually refers to substances made up of vegetable or animal matter free of human-produced chemicals.

PCBs—Polychlorinated biphenyls, heat-resistant compounds used in the manufacture of such products as fluorescent light fixtures and household appliances with electric capacitors.

PET—Polyethylene terephthalate, a type of plastic packaging material used for soda bottles.

plastic—A generic term for hundreds of different kinds of plastic materials.

photodegradable—Degrades or decomposes in sunlight.

pollute—To contaminate or make dirty by adding harmful substances.

polymer—A molecule made up of a long chain of units called monomers.

polystyrene foam—A plastic material used primarily for fast-food containers such as clam shells, cups, bowls, and trays.

radioactivity—The process by which atoms decay or change, emitting particles and rays.

PVC—Polyvinyl chloride (or vinyl), a type of plastic material used to make packaging products such as blister packs and pour spouts for vegetable oils.

recycling—Reusing waste materials.

resin—A material used to make a liquid solid.

resource recovery—The process of accumulating large amounts of waste and burning it in a huge incinerator to produce energy.

sanitary landfill—A solid waste disposal site designed to reduce hazards to the environment and human health.

solid waste—Garbage that waste haulers dispose of in landfills.

toxic—Poisonous.

vitrification—The process of heating various materials to turn them into glasslike substances.

windrow—A row of leaves left to decompose.

Index

A acid rain, 45, 89, 93, 97
aluminum, 6, 7, 18, 21, 22,
    30-31, 33, 34, 38-40,
    44, 69, 98, 99, 102
American Paper Institute, 24, 28
American Petroleum Institute,
    49
asbestos, 11, 12, 64
Asner, Ed, 37
atomic bomb, 79
Atomic Industrial Forum, 88
Avtex Fibers, 68

B bacteria, 7, 47, 49, 58-60, 75
Bahamas, 10
Baltimore, Md., 46
Bayh, Evan, 12
BDX Process, 48
Bhopal, India, 68, 94
biodegradable, 20, 58-60, 95,
    100
Borough of High Bridge, N.J.,
    22
bottles, 14, 18, 21, 22, 30, 55,
    56, 58, 59, 61
Brooklyn, N.Y., 10
Bush, President George, 85

C Canada, 6, 70, 80, 85, 86
carbon dioxide, 27
Center for Plastics Recycling, 56
Center Point Landfill, 11
Chernobyl, 90
Chevron, 62
Chicago, Ill., 21, 35, 36, 38

China, 26
chloroflurocarbons (CFCs),
    61-63
Clean Air Act, 45, 69, 95, 96
composting, 20, 47, 48, 93, 101
Coors, 67
cullet, 30

D Denver, Colo., 67, 83, 84
dioxin, 27, 45, 58
Dow Chemical, 60
dump (site), 7, 11, 13, 21, 49,
    65, 70, 76, 78, 83, 89

E Earth Care Paper, 100
Earth Day, 95-96
energy, 9, 23, 33, 44-47, 49,
    50, 53, 59, 79, 80, 82,
    88-91, 94
Environmental Defense Fund
    (EDF), 96, 102
Environmental Protection
    Agency (EPA), 14, 27,
    42, 50, 65-71, 75, 91,
    97, 98
Exxon Corporation, 75
Exxon Valdez, 49

F Federal Bureau of Investigation
    (FBI), 71, 84
ferrous scrap, 38, 39
Fina Oil, 62
fission, 79, 81, 82, 86
Four County Landfill, 70
France, 6, 54, 80, 85, 86
Friends of the Earth, 96

fuel rods, 81, 82

G Gallup Organization, 99
garbage, 1, 5-7, 9-15, 20-23,
    44, 46, 48, 50, 75, 78,
    81, 93, 100
Germany, 54, 59, 70, 86
Girl Scouts, 18, 96
Glass Container Industry, 30
gleaners, 31
Great Britain, 6, 70, 79
Greenpeace, 70, 75, 96, 99, 100

H Hanford Reservation, 79, 83,
    85
Harrelson, Lowell, 10
Hassenflug, Gerry, 73, 74
high-density polyethylene
    (HDPE), 56, 61, 62
Hewlett-Packard, 67
Honeywell, 67
HOPE, 11, 75, 99
humus, 20, 47
hydrogen, 57, 79, 80, 86

I IBM, 67
Institute of Scrap Recycling, 43
iron ore, 39, 40
Islip, N.Y., 10, 46
Italy, 6, 70, 86

J Japan, 14, 70, 80, 86
Jaycees, 18

K KAP, 97, 98, 102
Krulewitch, Simon, 36-37

L landfill, 7-14, 18, 21, 30, 42,
    46-49, 52, 60, 61, 66,
    67, 70, 71, 98, 99
LaPorte, Ind., 16
low-density polyethylene
    (LDPE), 56
leachate, 7, 8, 9, 66, 76
litter, 5, 30, 60
Love Canal, N.Y., 65

M Madison, Wis., 9, 59, 100

Martin Marietta, 83
McDonald's, 62, 63
methane, 9, 10
Mexico, 10, 70, 86
Midwest Research Institute, 58
Minneapolis, Minn., 59
Mobil, 62
Modesto, Cal., 53
Moore, Terri, 11
motor oil, 44, 49-51, 73

N National Polystyrene
    Recycling Company, 62
National Audubon Society, 96,
    99
National Wildlife Federation,
    69, 92, 96, 101
newsprint, 16, 20, 25, 27
NIMBY, 10, 79, 88
Nora, Nebr., 78, 88
Nuclear Regulatory
    Commission, 91
nuclear waste, 6, 46, 78-83,
    85-89, 91

O Oak Ridge, Tenn., 84
oil, 50, 51
    spill, 49
organophosphate, 74
OTA, 60, 66, 67, 74
Oxford Energy, 53
ozone, 27, 61, 93

P papermaking, 26
polyethylene terephthalate
    (PET), 56, 61
Philadelphia, Penn., 46
plastic, 14, 19-21, 27, 39, 46,
    55-62, 68, 94, 95, 98-101
plutonium, 79, 82, 84-86
Point Comfort, Tex., 68
Poland, 36
polychlorinated biphenyls
    (PCBs), 42, 68, 71, 75, 84
polymers, 57, 59

polypropylene, 56, 60
polystyrene, 19, 55, 61
polyvinyl chloride (PVC), 56
Port Authority, 25
Portland, Oreg., 19, 20, 25, 54, 93
Portsmouth, N.H., 44, 84
Prince William Sound, Alas., 49, 75
pulp, 25-28

R radioactive, 6, 66, 67, 78, 80-90
reactor, 81, 86, 90
Recycle America, 23
recycling, 13-40, 42, 50-52, 61, 62, 73, 77, 85, 93, 95-99, 102
Redding, Cal., 54
resins, 57, 59, 60-62, 88
Resource Conservation and Recovery Act, 50, 95
Rochester, Ind., 70
Rockwell International, 83
Rocky Flats, Colo., 5, 83, 84
Rutgers University, 56

S Savannah River, 79, 85, 86
scrap metal yard, 37
scrap metals, 34, 36, 38-40, 46
Seattle, Wash., 23
Seventh Generation, 100
Shenandoah River, 68
slurry, 27
Society of the Plastics Industry, 62
solid waste, 6, 8-11, 14, 16, 19, 23, 33, 34, 45-48, 52, 60, 81, 98
St. Paul, Minn., 58
steel, 18, 30, 34, 38-40, 44, 50, 54, 82, 85, 86
Storage Technology, 67
Sumter County, Fla., 48, 49
Superfund, 65, 66, 68, 74

SWEEP, 19, 47, 99

T Three Mile Island, 90
throwaways, 7, 16, 18, 21, 34, 40, 75, 101
tires, 6, 39, 44, 52-54
toxic compounds, 7, 84
toxic emissions, 45, 46, 68, 73
trash, 5-14, 20-23, 34, 44, 49, 61, 62, 64, 75, 78, 81, 93
Tucson, Ariz., 54

U U.S. Department of Transportation, 42
U.S. Office of Technology Assessment, 60. *See also* OTA
Union Carbide, 68, 94
Union of Concerned Scientists, 89
uranium, 79, 80-82, 84-86

V Ventura, Calif., 73
vitrification, 74, 85, 86

W Wal-Mart, 94
Warren County, W.Va., 68
Waste Isolation Pilot Plant, 86
waste management, 9, 10, 13, 22, 23, 48, 51, 52, 73, 77, 78, 93, 98
Waste Not Society, 98
Watkins, James. 85, 90
Westinghouse Corporation, 83
Weyerhaeuser, 25
Wilson, Tom, 14
windrows, 47, 48
Wisconsin Department of Natural Resources, 20
World War II, 37, 56, 79
Worldwatch Institute, 96
WOW, 25

Y Yucca Mountain, 87